W0235442

Personal Relationships and Intimacy in the Age of Social Media

Cristina Miguel

Personal Relationships and Intimacy in the Age of Social Media

palgrave
macmillan

Cristina Miguel
Business School
Leeds Beckett University
Leeds, UK

ISBN 978-3-030-02061-3   ISBN 978-3-030-02062-0   (eBook)
https://doi.org/10.1007/978-3-030-02062-0

Library of Congress Control Number: 2018959559

This Palgrave Pivot imprint is published by the registered company Springer Nature
Switzerland AG
The registered company address is: Gewerbestrasse 11, 6330 Cham, Switzerland

PREFACE

The development of digital technologies fosters specific forms of socialization, such as those afforded by social media platforms. Personal relationships in these platforms are dominated by dynamics that include trust, reputation, and visibility. As a result, real identities are increasingly represented online in mainstream social media (e.g., Facebook), thus relocating pre-established relationships (family, friends, work colleagues) into the social media environment. However, other social media platforms allow meeting new people online, where issues around authenticity, social stigma, and safety concerns arise. Most of the research about intimacy practices and privacy online have been focused on teenagers' or college students' use of social media (e.g., boyd 2010, 2014; Ito et al. 2009; Turkle 2011), particularly in mainstream social media platforms such as Facebook or MySpace. As a result, these studies were carried out mostly about intimacy practices within existing relationships. Some studies about digital media use within interpersonal relationships (Baym 2010), on self-disclosure via social media (Lomborg 2013; Pedroni et al. 2014), and about intimacy on Facebook (Lambert 2013) are a few examples of research about intimacy practices facilitated by social media among adults. There is still a lot to investigate about the types of personal interactions generated through social media. It is important to explore the workings of intimacy practices fostered by the use of these new technologies in order to help define characteristics of contemporary society. In addition, Baym (2011) argues, there is a need for more studies of adults, and their broad use of different kinds of social media (also social media platforms where people have contact with strangers), in order to fully comprehend the relationships between social media, privacy, and intimacy practices.

For doing this, it is important to pay attention to the social practices fostered by social media, both online and offline, across multiple platforms, for different nationalities and cultures. This study has been conducted in the UK and Spain. Although it would have been interesting to examine cultural differences in relation to intimacy practices through social media, the fact is that half of the participants were expats; therefore, I cannot claim that this is a comparative study between British and Spanish cultures. However, I can hypothesize that people who move to other countries tend to use social media to find new friends and partners more often than people who remain in the same location. In order to understand how online sociality has evolved, Van Dijck (2013) suggests looking at different social media platforms "as if they were *microsystems*" because each design and architecture cultivates a different style of connectedness, but altogether, they conform a unique ecosystem. Following Van Dijck (2013), I examine three different social media platforms—Badoo, CouchSurfing, and Facebook—in order to map this new social media ecosystem.

In particular, this study focuses on (mediated) intimacy practices among adults (25–49 years old) to analyse how users create and maintain intimate relationships through social media. The book aims to bring together a critical analysis of the politics of social media with users' perspectives by employing a multi-method research design, which combines interviews, participant observation, and the analysis of platforms' architecture and user profiles. The methodology is grounded on an ethnographic approach and is informed by feminist theory. The design of the study is cross-platform and multi-sited (UK and Spain). The sample is based on convenience sampling, and it is composed of 30 participants aged 25–49 years identified as users of Badoo or CouchSurfing located in Leeds (UK) and Barcelona (Spain). Participants' identity is protected by the use of pseudonyms. I collected the data through participant observation, in-depth interviews, and user profiles. The data was analysed through thematic analysis by triangulating the data gathered through different means.

The main aims of the book are to explore the characteristics of intimacy practices on social media and to question if intimacy online exists in spite of the publicity afforded in these platforms. For doing so, this research examines the extent to which participants expose their intimacy through social media, as well as the strategies they use to manage their privacy online. The research gathers users' perspectives on what constitutes intimate information (visual and textual) and how they negotiate its publication on social media. It explores the relationship between the architecture and politics of social media platforms, and the emergent intimacy practices that take place within them. The study also investigates whether participants consider that personal relationships originated via social media are shallower than relationships created in other environments; safety, authenticity, and social stigma concerns; as well as the extent patriarchal gender roles are reproduced online.

Leeds, UK   Cristina Miguel

References

Baym, N. K. (2010). *Personal connection in the digital age*. Cambridge: Polity Press.

Baym, N. K. (2011). Social networks 2.0. In M. Consalvo & C. Ess (Eds.), *The handbook of internet studies* (pp. 384–405). Oxford: Wiley-Blackwell.

boyd, d. (2010). Friendship. In M. Ito. et al. (Eds.), *Digital research confidential: The secrets of studying behavior online* (pp. 79–115). Cambridge, MA: MIT Press.

boyd, d. (2014). *It's complicated: The social lives of networked teens*. New Haven: Yale University Press.

Ito, M., Horst, H., Bittani, M., boyd, d., Herr-Stephenson, B., Lange, P. G., Pascoe, C. J., & Robinson, L. (2009). *Living and learning with new media: Summary of findings from the digital youth project*. Cambridge, MA: MIT Press.

Lambert, A. (2013). *Intimacy and friendship on Facebook*. Basingstoke: Palgrave Macmillan.

Lomborg, S. (2013). *Social media, social genres: Making sense of the ordinary*. New York: Routledge.

Pedroni, M., Pasquali, F., & Carlo, S. (2014). My friends are my audience: Mass-mediation of personal content and relations in Facebook. *Observatorio (OBS*)*, *8*(3), 97–113.

Turkle, S. (2011). *Alone together: Why we expect more from technology and less from each other*. New York: Basic Books.

Van Dijck, J. (2013). *The culture of connectivity: A critical history of social media*. Oxford: Oxford University Press.

ACKNOWLEDGEMENTS

First, I thank Dr. Pilar Medina and Dr. Lluís Codina, as they provided me with the inchoate inspiration for this project. I express my gratitude to Dr. Nancy Thumim, for her continuous support throughout this research journey, especially for her patience, motivation, and positive feedback. I also thank the other scholars who provided me with support at various stages of this study at the University of Leeds: Prof. Helen Kennedy and Prof. Stephen Coleman. Additionally, this research project has gained much from the three months that I spent at the University of West England as a visiting scholar, under the direction of Prof. Adam Joinson.

I thank my colleagues for stimulating discussions. In particular, I thank Salem, Andreas, and Mario for listening to my thoughts and helping me to better articulate my research findings.

Finally, I thank all the participants in this research project. Without their collaboration, this study would have been impossible. Participants, you have shared with me sometimes quite personal stories in order to contribute to an understanding of intimacy practices in the age of social media. Thank you!

CONTENTS

CONTENTS

CHAPTER 1

Introduction

Abstract This chapter explores the values and history of network culture, the commercial turn of the Internet, the field of Internet studies, and how social media platforms mediate communication in order to contextualize the study of intimacy in the age of social media. It introduces the concept of intimacy in digital contexts by discussing the tensions between privacy and publicity on social media interaction, as well as the interplay between the politics of platforms and the intimacy practices that take place through them. Finally, it presents an outline of the content of the rest of the chapters.

Keywords Internet history • Internet studies • Intimacy • Network culture • Social media

1.1 Networked Culture

The way we establish, maintain, modify, or destroy social relations, according to Castells (2004), has changed to a new social paradigm in the late twentieth century: the network society. Castells (ibid.) points to a communication paradigm shift as a result of the advent of the Internet, the economic crisis, and different social movements such as feminism and ecologism. Likewise, Rossiter (2006) observes that "the network" has been one of the most used metaphors in picturing this new social structure, based on connections of practices and information through the Net.

© The Author(s) 2018
C. Miguel, *Personal Relationships and Intimacy in the Age of Social Media*, https://doi.org/10.1007/978-3-030-02062-0_1

1

In order to approach the study of network culture, I start by analysing how the Internet was first configured and how it was transformed through the years by the influences of different countercultures, economic forces, and practices. In this section, I also discuss how the use of the Internet became mainstream with the emergence of social media services.

The telegraph has been considered the precursor of the Internet. Nevertheless, rather than to facilitate personal communication, the Internet was originally developed for military purposes. The Internet was created by the US Defense Department in the 1960s, as several scholars (e.g., Castells 2001; Curran 2012) have addressed. The Defense Advance Research Projects Agency (DARPA) created a network of computers that could still transmit information to each other despite being attacked. DARPA evolved under the Advanced Research Projects Agency Network (ARPANET), a research network that also included the think tank corporation RAND, the Massachusetts Institute of Technology (MIT), and the National Physics Laboratory (NPL) from the UK. Later the University of California, Los Angeles (UCLA), and Stanford University joined the project. Those academics who created the technical mechanisms to allow electronic communication also developed the protocols for interpersonal communications. Following this argument, Castells (2001) analyses the values of the network culture using a historical perspective and argues that at least four distinct cultures have shaped the Internet: (1) techno-elites (academics, innovators, and early adopters), (2) hacker culture (*open-source* movement), (3) virtual communitarians (roots in the San Francisco Bay area's countercultures), and (4) entrepreneurs (Silicon Valley).

Castells (ibid.) explains that the network culture is based on the academic tradition of sharing knowledge, reputation derived from academic excellence, peer review, and openness in all findings obtained through research. Historically, the Internet was developed in academia, by the work of both teachers and students, whose values, habits, and knowledge spread in the hacker culture. Lévy (2001) describes in his book *Cyberculture*, which takes a philosophical approach of his own experiences as an Internet user, the characteristics of cyberspace and the social relations that emanate from this new environment. For Lévy (ibid.), hacker culture refers to the set of values and beliefs that emerged from the networks of computer programmers interacting online to collaborate on projects of creative programming. Yet Castells (2001) argues that the specific values and social organization of hacker culture are best understood if one considers the development of the *open-source* movement, where the operating system

Linux is one of its main examples. The hacker culture shares characteristics of the techno-meritocratic culture with the academic world, but has a countercultural character that makes it different. Freedom is the supreme value of hacker culture. Freedom combined with collaboration through the practice of *gift culture*, which means that a hacker publishes their contribution to the development of software in the network with the expectation of reciprocity and recognition. In summary, hacker culture is a culture of technological creativity based on freedom, cooperation, reciprocity, and informality. Based on the values of hacker culture, as Barbrook (1998) observes, users collaborate altruistically within a system where there is no monetary exchange, what he labels the *hi-tech gift economy*.

In the same vein, Castells (2001) stresses that network culture is not only reduced to the values of technological innovation, but it also includes social patterns. So while hacker culture provides the technological foundations of the Internet, community culture, manifested in social forms, provides the processes and uses. Early users of computer networks created virtual communities and these communities were sources of values, patterns of behaviour, and social organization. Virtual communities, continues Castells (ibid.), have their roots in the counterculture movements of the 1960s, especially the hippie communes. In the 1970s, the San Francisco Bay area was the site of many virtual communities that experimented with computer-mediated communication (CMC), where projects such as the *Community Memory project* (1973) and *Homebrew Computer Club* (1975) developed. The *Community Memory project* was the first *bulletin board system*. Those involved in *Usenet* news networks and the *bulletin board system* developed and disseminated forms and network applications: messaging, mailing lists, chat channels, multiuser games, and conferences. Communities of interests were created around these new communication channels. These virtual communities were characterized by free horizontal communication and the ability for anyone to express their opinions. Rheingold (1993) introduced the term virtual community into the public lexicon with his book *The Virtual Community: Homesteading on the Electronic Frontier*, where he gathered his experiences participating in the virtual community "The WELL". As virtual communities were expanding in size and scope, the original connection with counterculture weakened.

Later, Wellman and Gulia (1997), in their article "Net Surfers Don't Ride Alone: Virtual Communities as Communities", criticized the use of the term "virtual community" and pointed to the use of the concept "social networks" in order to picture the relationship created among

Internet users through bulletin boards and forums. In opposition to traditional forms of community (the neighbourhood, the family, the school), Rainie and Wellman (2012, p. 3) suggest that the Internet facilitates the creation of different social networks around the individual. Rainie and Wellman (ibid.) have developed the concept of *networked individualism*, where the individual is a connectivity node who administers diverse social networks. Although Californian counterculture values influenced the configuration of the network culture, according to Castells (2001), the hacker culture plays an essential role in building it for two reasons: the hacker culture is a breeding ground for technology through cooperation and free communication innovations, and it bridges the knowledge generated in the techno-meritocratic culture with entrepreneurship start-ups that spread Internet use in wider society. Start-ups were mainly concentrated around Silicon Valley (California) and created what was labelled the dot. com bubble, which burst in the early 2000s. Castells (2001) argues that there was certain distrust with the commercialization of the Internet at that time. On the other hand, Curran (2012) observes that these dot.com start-ups had very unrealistic business plans. Nevertheless, Fuchs (2014) points to the low number of Internet users at the end of the 1990s as the main cause of the failure of most of these projects. Fuchs (ibid.) explains how Web 2.0 emerged after the dot.com crisis in order to create new Internet business models and ways of monetizing traffic, where the main source of value comes from the users who co-create content.

With the emergence of the World Wide Web in the 1990s, Internet-related research began to emerge to explore the new social relations facilitated by this medium. Some of these studies were located under the umbrella of the so-called field of CMC, defined by Ess (2012, p. 276) as "studies rooted both in social science and disciplines such as sociology, and anthropology, and in humanistic disciplines, such as linguistics, literature, and media, and communication studies". CMC studies focused on online social interaction through MOOs,[1] forums, and "virtual communities" (e.g., Turkle 1995; Wellman and Gulia 1997; Markham 1998; Baym 1999). For instance, Markham (1998), in her study of MOOs, observed that the Internet could be considered a place to go, a tool, or a way of being. At this time, terms such as cyberspace, cyborg, and virtual/real

---

[1] MOO (multi-object oriented) is a type of MUD (multi-user dimension) program that allows people to interact simultaneously within virtual communities (Markham 1998).

were discussed. In particular, the figure of the cyborg, that androgynous mix between human and machine that Haraway (1985) described in her famous manifesto, appeared as an aspirational metaphor to convey the increasing integration of technology in everyday life. The cyborg, half-human and half-machine, which did not have gender assigned, could help people, especially women, to escape from a gender-ruled society. In the mid-1990s the word "cyberfeminism" gained popularity. Haraway (1985, 1997) and Plant (1997) were the most prominent utopian cyberfeminist scholars who argued that the Internet was a tool that might liberate and empower women. As Rosser (2005, p. 17) observes, "cyberfeminism explored the ways that information technologies and the Internet provide avenues to liberate (or oppress) women".

In recent years the extensive adoption of Internet use and the boom of social media have moved the discussion from cyberculture to everyday practices (e.g., Bakardjieva 2005; Cohen 2012; Pink 2012; Hine 2015). In the 2000s, anthropologists (e.g., Hine 2000; Miller and Slater 2000) started to conduct ethnographies about "cyberculture". These and other media scholars (e.g., Lévy 2001; Lessig 2006) moved the discussion from the virtual/real to the online/offline dichotomy. Nowadays, the meta-phors used to explain the hybridity of the digital medium have changed. For instance, Floridi (2012, p. 271) suggests the term *onlife* to define the "infosphere that is neither entirely virtual nor only physical". Concepts such as "co-presence" (Hjorth 2014, p. 52), "always on" (Baron 2008, p. 10; Turkle 2008, p. 132), "being-as-mediated" (Kember and Zylinska 2012, p. 40), and "lifestreaming" (Marwick 2013, p. 205) are also useful to understand the pervasiveness of mediated communication in our every-day life and how this ubiquitous social media interaction affects personal relationships and intimacy.

Located in the field of Internet studies, this book aims to contribute to the understanding of how people build intimacy and manage privacy on social media interaction, with a focus on adults (25–49 years old). The project attempts to engage with the general questions about intimacy and relationships that social media brings to academic and political debates. I investigate the intimate experiences of social media users in different con-texts by using a cross-platform approach (for an extended discussion of my methods, see Miguel 2016). I map and compare the different kinds of intimacy practices that participants experience through three social media platforms of different genres: Badoo (dating/hook-up platform), CouchSurfing (hospitality exchange/meet-up platform), and Facebook (generalist platform), although I also discuss other dating/hook-up platforms, such as Meetic, AdultFriendFinder, or AdoptaUnTio (AdoptAGuy), in a few occasions. Given that these platforms facilitate offline interaction, I explore personal interactions both online and offline. CouchSurfing and Badoo provide interactions between strangers, and Facebook is mainly used to connect with known others. This is useful to map the diverse intimate interactions facilitated by social media platforms that can take place within both new and existing relationships. The analysis and comparison of data gathered through participant observation, interviews, and user profiles provide empirical examples of intimacy practices (both online and offline) facilitated by the use of social media. In order to provide background to this debate, the concept of intimacy needs to be discussed in the context of social media.

1.2   INTIMACY IN DIGITAL CONTEXTS

Intimacy is a concept that seems to be valued more and more in contemporary society, as Chambers (2006, p. 14) explains: "The economic, cultural and political destabilisation of traditional community values coincide with the ascendance of intimacy, privacy and the project of the self." Bauman (2003) suggests that in individualistic Western societies, people tend to feel lost, as their lives are not primarily organized around traditional social structures, such as religion or community. The loss of community support can make people feel disappointed about the uncertainty of the future. On the other hand, in this so-called *hyperindividualistic* society (Vidal 1992), Bauman (2003, p. xiii) identifies the tensions between the desire for freedom and the need for social bonds, of living "together, and apart". Bauman (2003) suggests that people change tight bonds for networks, and quality for quantity in an ever-ending mobile and transient life path, where settling down becomes a hard task. Following this debate, Rainie and Wellman (2012, p. 3) argue that *networked individualism* is the new social operating system, where individuals participate in different networks, which creates a different social structure where people are geographically dispersed, in opposition to traditional local communities. In this context, Chambers (2013) suggests that social media platforms fit neatly into this constant self-updating process, insofar as they allow self-expression, but they also facilitate the negotiation of different kinds of relationships. This opens up important questions about the role of social media platforms in negotiating intimacy in everyday life, which I explore in this book.

Increasingly, the extensive use of social media, according to Ito et al. (2009), is fostering the habit of individuals defining themselves by what they can show and what others can see. There is a current debate around how social media affect the notions of privacy and intimacy. The traditional belief that the development of intimacy requires privacy (e.g., Gerstein 1984; Turkle 2011) is questioned by the new intimacy practices online. Some authors consider that intimacy through social media ceases to be intimacy and becomes something else (e.g., Sibilia 2008; Turkle 2011; Madianou and Miller 2013), or it is illusory (e.g., Van Manen 2010; Taddicken and Jers 2011). Madianou and Miller (2013, p. 174) note that by using social media to negotiate intimacy, a new phenomenon is created "of different scale, affective resonance and consequences".

Other scholars (e.g., boyd 2008; Papacharissi and Gibson 2011; Van Dijck 2013) highlight that the broadcasting afforded by social media services largely augments the scope of the information published online, and these platforms are actually designed to foster self-disclosure. It is established that technology is not neutral but cultivates particular kinds of interactions (e.g., Papacharissi 2009; Gillespie 2010; Van Dijck 2013). For example, through public-by-default settings configuration, social media platforms make exposure easier than privacy. Hine (2015) highlights the importance of criticizing social media platforms' design and making their infrastructures visible in order to understand how they exercise power over users. She considers it useful to study the connection between socio-technical features and lived experiences to explore how users appropriate the use of technology in their everyday lives.

Most popular social media platforms encourage sharing because they involve disclosure of personal information to foster interaction with other users (Joinson et al. 2011), but they also promote sharing to gather users' data for profit (e.g., Van Dijck 2013; Kennedy 2013). In this context, Mancinelli and Mancinelli (2013, p. 161) analyse how Facebook claims that their service is free and that they will never charge for the service in order to hide their actual commodification of users: "If you cannot see the price, you are the commodity." Hence, a double logic of empowerment and commodification is identified in social media interaction, as observed by Hinton and Hjorth (2013). Lomborg and Bechmann (2014, p. 4) highlight that in order to understand this double social media logic, it is necessary to combine users' and industry perspectives, as they put it: "to elicit deep analysis of how user productivity and behavioural patterns may add value chain of online business models while at the same time offering significant personal reward and pleasure for the users". Drawing on Baym (2010), I acknowledge two interactive forces which shape the way people communicate through social media: (1) social media platforms that have particular affordances and politics which allow certain kinds of interactions, and (2) actual practices of use, as people appropriate these platforms in different ways to negotiate diverse types of personal relationships in everyday life. In recent studies, scholars have examined the conditions of production of social media (e.g., Couldry 2012; Van Dijck 2013; Fuchs 2014). There are also studies that explore what people *do* with this technology (e.g., Bakardjieva 2005; Baym 2010; boyd 2014). In order to fully comprehend the social media platforms that form part of the current digital media ecology, it is necessary to study not only users' practices and the content they produce, but also socio-technical features and business models (e.g., Van Dijck 2009; Lomborg and Bechmann 2014; Stanfill 2014). As Couldry (2012) observes, it is important to analyse what people do through media interaction; however, media research that does not acknowledge political economy is incomplete. For this reason, in this book, I also analyse social media platforms' politics and business models, which are tied to the affordances and services that they provide, and hence to the intimacy practices that emerge from their use.

1.3   Outline of the Book

So far in this chapter, I have analysed the origins of the values of network culture(s), which are rooted in the meritocratic academic culture where the Internet was first expanded; the hacker culture and its collaborative and free values based on the gift economy; the counterculture movements from the 1960s and 1970s in the San Francisco Bay area, which revolved around communitarianism, peace, altruism, and collaboration; and the start-up culture developed in the same area (although more focused on the Silicon Valley), characterized by entrepreneurial spirit. In this context, I have addressed the commercial turn of the Web. Later I have provided some background information about the concept on intimacy in the context of social media, a topic which I will explore further in Chap. 2. Hereafter, I summarize the content of the rest of the book.

The objective of Chap. 2 is to present the conceptual framework to approach the study of intimacy through social media, which includes the following topics: an introduction to the concept of intimacy; a discussion about the relationships between intimacy and privacy; an exploration of what happens to the traditional concept of intimacy when intimacy is mediated through social media and whether the concept needs to be redefined in social media contexts; and following this debate, it explores further the notion of intimacy in public. The aim of this chapter is to provide a theoretical framework to discuss the way people negotiate new and existing relationships through social media, and how the notion of intimacy is affected by social media interaction.

In Chap. 3, I identify self-disclosure and self-(re)presentation as a necessary part for developing intimate relationships online. I analyse what participants considered intimate information in the context of social media interaction, which mostly revolves around sexual orientation and relationship status (whether they were in a relationship or not and with whom). Other intimate topics would be sex, alcohol, emotions, and political or religious beliefs. It is interesting to note that the definition of what is intimate or not is contextual—dependent on the platform used, one particular intimate information may be considered appropriate to disclose or not. For instance, sexual orientation was not often disclosed on Facebook, while it was always revealed on Badoo, where it seemed appropriate in that context. I analyse how participants negotiate the disclosure of intimate information both through textual and visual means of communication. In this context, the co-creation of identity by our contacts causes a loss of control over the construction of one's online identity. For instance, participants often expressed concern about photos they appeared in being published by their contacts.

The aim of Chap. 4 is to understand how social media platforms shape the way people communicate and negotiate personal relationships. I first give a historical account of social media. Then, I move on to discuss the issue of mediation, particularly in the context of social media interaction within personal relationships. Later, I examine the way that platforms' architecture and politics shape the way people communicate and develop personal relationships. In the following sections, I analyse online dating and hospitality exchange platforms, using Badoo and CouchSurfing as case studies, respectively. I focus the attention on their architecture and affordances. For example, CouchSurfing and Badoo provide reputation and verification systems to build trust among the users. This is connected to their business models because the user's identity is verified by paying a fee to CouchSurfing, and by purchasing premium services on Badoo.

In Chap. 5, I address the culture of participation and the workings of Web 2.0 technology, with a special focus on the political economy of these platforms. I analyse the role of social media companies that encourage users to share personal information to connect with others, but at the same time, mine this data for profit. I explore how these companies have mobilized the concept of sharing to promote user disclosure of intimate information. Following Hinton and Hjorth's (2013) notion that social media both control and empower users, I argue that social media platforms operate under "a double logic of empowerment and commodification". In this sense, social media platforms are tools that provide a great means of communication, but at the same time, they may be used to control users. I examine the business models of Badoo, Couchsurfing, and Facebook to see how they affect intimacy practices. In addition, I discuss the issue of commodification from two perspectives—the commodification of personal relationships by social media services through their business models (e.g., customized advertising, charging an access fee) and the self-commodification of users to promote themselves in the network—to analyse to what extent it is considered anti-normative.

In Chap. 6, I focus on the practice of meeting new people online. I examine authenticity issues, the risks, and the stigma associated with this practice. In addition, I discuss how traditional gender roles are reproduced through social media interactions, especially on Badoo, despite some feminist scholars' claims in the 1990s about the potential liberating effect of the Internet, where gender roles could be reversed. In the last section, I explore how people move relationships offline. I emphasize that intimate relationships created through social media, even if temporary, are valued positively, especially in the case of friendships created through CouchSurfing.

Finally, in Chap. 7, I present my conclusions. I synthesize all the empirical findings and consolidate all the important issues raised across the discussion.

REFERENCES

Bakardjieva, M. (2005). *Internet society: The Internet in everyday life.* London: Sage Publications.

Barbrook, R. (1998). The hi-tech gift economy. *First Monday, 3*(12). http://journals.uic.edu/ojs/index.php/fm/article/view/631/552. Date Accessed 10 Oct 2013.

Baron, N. (2008). *Always on: Language in an online and mobile world*. Oxford: Oxford University Press.

Bauman, Z. (2003). *Liquid love: On the frailty of human bonds*. Cambridge: Polity Press.

Baym, N. K. (1999). *Tune in, log on: Soaps, fandom, and online community*. Thousand Oaks: Sage Publications.

Baym, N. K. (2010). *Personal connection in the digital age*. Cambridge: Polity Press.

boyd, d. (2008). Facebook's privacy trainwreck: Exposure, invasion, and social convergence. *Convergence, 14*(1), 13–20.

boyd, d. (2014). *It's complicated: The social lives of networked teens*. New Haven: Yale University Press.

Castells, M. (2001). *The Internet galaxy: Reflections on the Internet, business and society*. Oxford: Oxford University Press.

Castells, M. (2004). *The network society: A cross-cultural perspective*. Northampton: Edward Elgar.

Chambers, D. (2006). *New social ties: Contemporary connections in a fragmented society*. Basingstoke: Palgrave Macmillan.

Chambers, D. (2013). *Social media and personal relationships: Online intimacies and networked friendship*. Basingstoke: Palgrave Macmillan.

Cohen, J. E. (2012). *Configuring the networked self: Law, code, and the play of everyday practice*. New Have: Yale University Press.

Couldry, N. (2012). *Media, society, world: Social theory and digital media practice*. Cambridge: Polity Press.

Curran, J. (2012). Rethinking Internet history. In J. Curran, N. Fenton, & D. Freedman (Eds.), *Misunderstanding the Internet* (pp. 3–33). London: Routledge.

Ess, C. (2012). At the intersections between Internet studies and philosophy: "Who am I online?". *Philosophy & Technology, 25*(3), 275–284.

Floridi, L. (2012). Technologies of the self. *Philosophy & Technology, 25*(3), 271–273.

Fuchs, C. (2014). *Social media: A critical introduction*. London: Sage Publications.

Gerstein, R. (1984). Intimacy and privacy. In F. Schoeman (Ed.), *Philosophical dimensions of privacy: An anthology* (pp. 265–271). Cambridge: Cambridge University Press.

Gillespie, T. (2010). The politics of "platforms". *New Media & Society, 12*(3), 347–364.

Haraway, D. (1985). A manifesto for cyborgs: Science, technology and socialist-feminism in the 1980s. *Socialist Review, 15*(2), 65–107.

Haraway, D. (1997). *Modest_Witness@Second_Millennium.FemaleMan©Meets_OncoMouse™: Feminism and technoscience*. New York: Routledge.

Hine, C. (2000). *Virtual ethnography*. London: Sage Publications.

Hine, C. (2015). *Ethnography for the Internet: Embedded, embodied and everyday.* London: Bloomsbury Publishing.

Hinton, S., & Hjorth, L. (2013). *Understanding social media.* London: Sage Publications.

Hjorth, L. (2014). Co-presence and ambient play: A case study of mobile gaming. In M. Berry & M. Schleser (Eds.), *Mobile media making in an age of smartphones* (pp. 48–57). New York: Palgrave Pivot.

Ito, M., Horst, H., Bittani, M., boyd, d., Herr-Stephenson, B., Lange, P. G., Pascoe, C. J., & Robinson, L. (2009). *Living and learning with new media: Summary of findings from the digital youth project.* Cambridge, MA: MIT Press.

Joinson, A. N., Houghton, D. J., Vasalou, A., & Marder, B. L. (2011). Digital crowding: Privacy, self-disclosure, and technology. In S. Trepte & L. Reinecke (Eds.), *Privacy online: Perspectives on privacy and self-disclosure in the social web* (pp. 33–45). Heidelberg: Springer.

Kember, S., & Zylinska, J. (2012). *Life after new media: Mediation as a vital process.* Cambridge, MA: MIT Press.

Kennedy, J. (2013). Rhetorics of sharing: Data, imagination, and desire. In G. Lovink & M. Rasch (Eds.), *Unlike us reader: Social media monopolies and their alternatives* (pp. 127–136). Amsterdam: Institute of Network Cultures.

Lessig, L. (2006). *Code: Version 2.0.* London: Basic Books.

Lévy, P. (2001). *Cyberculture.* Minneapolis: University of Minnesota Press.

Lomborg, S., & Bechmann, A. (2014). The ubiquitous Internet: Introduction and conceptualization. In A. Bechmann & S. Lomborg (Eds.), *The ubiquitous Internet: User and industry perspectives* (pp. 1–5). London: Routledge.

Madianou, M., & Miller, D. (2013). Polymedia: Towards a new theory of digital media in interpersonal communication. *International Journal of Cultural Studies, 16*(2), 169–187.

Mancinelli, I., & Mancinelli, T. (2013). The Facebook aquarium: Freedom in a profile. In G. Lovink & M. Rasch (Eds.), *Unlike us reader: Social media monopolies and their alternatives* (pp. 159–165). Amsterdam: Institute of Network Cultures.

Markham, A. N. (1998). *Life online: Researching real experience in virtual space.* Walnut Creek: Rowman Altamira.

Marwick, A. E. (2013). *Status update: Celebrity, publicity, and branding in the social media age.* New Haven: Yale University Press.

Miguel, C. (2016). Researching intimacy through social media: A cross-platform approach. *Medie Kultur: The Journal of Communication Research, 32*(60), 50–69, 159–178.

Miller, D., & Slater, D. (2000). *The Internet: An ethnographic approach.* London: Berg.

Papacharissi, Z. (2009). The virtual geographies of social networks: A comparative analysis of Facebook, LinkedIn and ASmallWorld. *New Media & Society, 11*(1–2), 199–220.

Papacharissi, Z., & Gibson, P. L. (2011). Fifteen minutes of privacy: Privacy, sociability and publicity on social networks sites. In S. Trepte & L. Reinecke (Eds.), *Privacy online: Perspective on privacy and self-disclosure on the social web* (pp. 75–89). New York: Springer.

Pink, S. (2012). *Situating everyday life: Practices and places*. London: Sage Publications.

Plant, S. (1997). *Zeroes and ones: Digital women and the new technoculture*. London: Fourth Estate.

Rainie, H., & Wellman, B. (2012). *Networked: The new social operating system*. Cambridge, MA: MIT Press.

Rheingold, H. (1993). *The virtual community: Homesteading on the electronic frontier*. Cambridge, MA: MIT Press.

Rosser, S. V. (2005). Through the lenses of feminist theory: Focus on women and information technology. *Frontiers: A Journal of Women Studies, 26*(1), 1–23.

Rossiter, N. (2006). *Organized networks: Media theory, creative labour, new institutions*. Rotterdam: NAI Publications.

Sibilia, P. (2008). *La intimidad como espectáculo*. Buenos Aires: Fondo de Cultura Económica.

Stanfill, M. (2014). The interface as discourse: The production of norms through web design. *New Media & Society, 17*(7), 1059–1074.

Taddicken, M., & Jers, C. (2011). The uses of privacy online: Trading a loss of privacy for social web gratifications? In S. Trepte & L. Reinecke (Eds.), *Privacy online: Perspective on privacy and self-disclosure on the social web* (pp. 143–158). New York: Springer.

Turkle, S. (1995). *Life on the screen: Identity in the age of the Internet*. New York: Simon & Schuster Paperbacks.

Turkle, S. (2008). Always-on/always-on-you: The tethered self. In J. E. Katz (Ed.), *Handbook of mobile communication studies* (pp. 121–137). Cambridge, MA: MIT Press.

Turkle, S. (2011). *Alone together: Why we expect more from technology and less from each other*. New York: Basic Books.

Van Dijck, J. (2009). Users like you? Theorizing agency in user-generated content. *Media, Culture, and Society, 3*(1), 41–58.

Van Dijck, J. (2013). *The culture of connectivity: A critical history of social media*. Oxford: Oxford University Press.

Van Manen, M. (2010). The pedagogy of momus technologies: Facebook, privacy, and online intimacy. *Qualitative Health Research, 20*(8), 1023–1032.

Vidal, M. (1992). *Conceptos fundamentales de ética teológica*. Madrid: Editorial Trotta.

Wellman, B., & Gulia, M. (1997). Net surfers don't ride alone: Virtual communities as communities. In B. Wellman (Ed.), *Networks in the global village* (pp. 331–366). London: Perseus.

CHAPTER 2

Intimacy Frameworks in the Context of Social Media

Abstract This chapter presents an intimacy conceptual framework, discussing a number of concepts related to intimacy mediated through social media. First, the definition of intimacy is approached from different disciplines (e.g., philosophy, sociology, psychology). Then, the chapter elaborates in the often overlapping terms of privacy and intimacy. It questions whether the concept of intimacy needs to be redefined with the advance of digital communication and addresses the topic of public intimacy through social media platforms. The opinions and experiences of social media users are also introduced to contribute to these debates.

Keywords Intimacy • Personal relationships • Privacy • Public intimacy • Social media

2.1 INTRODUCTION

The main aim of this chapter is to explore the concept of intimacy in the context social media interaction to question if it *really exists* (Baym 2010; Jamieson 2013; Lambert 2013), if it is *redefined* (Sibilia 2008; Turkle 2011), or if it is *illusory* (Van Manen 2010; Taddicken and Jers 2011). First, I approach intimacy definitions and dimensions (physical, informational, and emotional) in order to approach my "starting point" concept of intimacy in the research project. Then, I focus on the interpretation of the concept of intimacy in the age of social media by participants: how

© The Author(s) 2018
C. Miguel, *Personal Relationships and Intimacy in the Age of Social Media*, https://doi.org/10.1007/978-3-030-02062-0_2

participants describe the concept of intimacy, which ways participants believe that intimacy is affected by social media affordances, and how participants understand intimacy practices performed in public when interacting through social media.

2.2   THE CONCEPT OF INTIMACY

There are different definitions of the concept of intimacy (e.g., Fried 1968; Giddens 1992; Inness 1996; Jamieson 1998; Berlant 2000; Zelizer 2009; Marar 2012). Nevertheless, the first and more extensive definition of intimacy, according to the *Oxford English Dictionary* (2015), is as follows:

> The quality or condition of "being intimate", and it includes three different meanings:
>
> (1) the state of being personally intimate; intimate friendship or acquaintance; familiar intercourse; close familiarity; an instance of this;
> (2) *euphem.* for sexual intercourse;
> (3) Closeness of observation, knowledge, or the like.

Following this definition, Zelizer (2009) identifies three different dimensions of intimacy: physical, informational, and emotional, although she notes that they may be interconnected and complement each other.

Building on Morgan's (2011) concept of "family practices", Jamieson (2012) introduces the term "practices of intimacy" to refer to "practices which enable, generate and sustain a subjective sense of closeness and being attuned and special to each other". Some scholars (e.g., Fried 1968; Giddens 1992; Plummer 2003; Marar 2012) define intimacy as related to the act of mutual sharing of inner thoughts and feelings. Marar (2012, p. 49) argues that intimacy is intrinsically reciprocal as it involves knowledge of each other and mutuality: "Intimacy exists *between* rather than within people; you can experience unrequited love, but you cannot experience unrequited intimacy". Likewise, Jamieson (2012) states that "love" and "intimacy" are close relatives, but she emphasizes that although expressing feelings of love may build intimacy, feelings of love can occur without reciprocity, whereas intimacy always refers to some form of interpersonal connections acknowledged by both parties as a relationship. Although some professional relationships may be intimate (i.e., prostitute-client, doctor-patient), meaningful relationships (based on love or friendship, for instance), the intimate relationships we value for their own sake, are the realm where intimacy usually flourishes. Likewise, Berlant (2000, p. 1) argues that intimacy involves a shared story, which is usually experienced in the context of loving relationships: "within zones of familiarity and comfort: friendship, the couple, and the family form, animated by expressive and emancipating kinds of love". Jamieson (2012) adds casual sexual relationships to the list of types of relationships where intimacy may arise because, she argues, intimacy can also be physical, bodily intimacy, although sexual contact can occur without intimacy. Jamieson (2012) agrees with Reiman (1976), Inness (1996), Berlant (2000), and Plummer (2003) in the need for some kind of liking or love in order to call a relationship "intimate", but she does not believe that all intimate relationships involve caring and sharing. Thus, Jamieson (1998, p. 13) affirms: "Intimacy involves close association, privileged knowledge, deep knowing and understanding and some form of love, but it need not include practical caring and sharing." Zelizer (2009), for instance, explains that there are certain types of negative intimacy that definitely do not involve caring, such as abusive sexual relations or malicious gossip.

Intimacy lies in the edge between vulnerability and support. Zelizer (2009, p. 34) points out that intimacy involves particularized knowledge such as "shared secrets, interpersonal rituals, bodily information, awareness of personal vulnerability, and shared memory of embarrassing situations", but also attention by other person(s), which includes, inter alia, bodily services, private languages, and emotional support. Reis and Shaver (1988) developed the interpersonal process model of intimacy (IPMI) framework, which is based on the notion that intimacy is achieved and enhanced through mutual intimate self-disclosure and validation. Other scholars (e.g., Shaffer and Tomarelli 1989) also examined how self-disclosure recipients are more likely to engage in the same practice as they feel the need to reciprocate with an equally intimate disclosure. Derlega and Berg (1987) suggest that equity social norms, based on the quid pro quo principle, would foster mutual intimate self-disclosure and help to develop intimacy, even among complete strangers. Nevertheless, they pointed out that if intimacy would only be based on mutual self-disclosure, both terms would be synonymous. Hence, Derlega and Berg (ibid.) state that what actually powers the intimacy process is that the information shared is valued by both the discloser and the recipient. Marar (2012, p. 10) highlights that intimacy requires a "degree of exposure or vulnerability that could be betrayed". For instance, in the context of social media interaction, as Garde-Hansen and Gorton (2013, p. 43) observe, "those loved have the power to exploit that intimacy online". For this reason, Marar (2012) suggests, some people may be tempted to "play safe" and not to get involved in intimate relationships. Giddens (1992) argues that personal boundaries are necessary to negotiate intimacy, in order to find a balance between openness, vulnerability, and trust. I return to the question of trust in mediated environments in Chap. 6.

On the other hand, the value and substance of intimacy are often located (e.g. Fried 1968; Reiman 1976; Garzón 2003; Marar 2012) in being an exclusive, scarce, restricted commodity. Marar (2012) states that intimacy is exclusive; that is, it exists between two people and excludes others. He acknowledges that his position is controversial because it implies that intimacy does not really exist within groups. Jamieson (2013), on the other hand, sustains that gregarious intimacy exists, that "groupal" intimacy may be experienced within a group of friends, but it still would be exclusive for that group. Fried (1968) describes intimacy's informational dimension as "the sharing of information about one's actions, beliefs, or emotions which one does not share with all, and which one has the right not to share with anyone" (1968, p. 211). Thus, intimacy is also, as David (2009) put it, "our secret garden" (2009, p. 79), which includes our dreams, desires, and fantasies. Some authors (e.g., Fried 1968; Reiman 1976; Garzón 2003) argue that intimacy has traditionally been experienced in the private realm. Garzón (2003) explains that there are certain kinds of behaviours people prefer to perform without witnesses or with selected relationships within the private sphere. This traditional association between privacy and intimacy made some participants confused about the border between the two. During the first stages of the fieldwork I realized that some participants mixed up the concepts of privacy and intimacy. In order to explore how the clash of both concepts occurs, in the next section I present privacy and intimacy definitions provided by participants, and discuss when a clash between the two concepts was expressed.

2.3   Disentangling Privacy and Intimacy?

The concept of privacy was mainly defined as non-disclosure, secrecy, confidentiality, opposite to public, related to the control over personal information, or non-interference in one's own space. On the other hand, the concept of intimacy was mainly defined within privacy, as closeness (emotional connection), physical (sexual, touching, looking in the eye), exclusive (restricted to a small circle), and dependent on trust. Constraining to reveal personal information was often included in participants' privacy definitions. Many participants defined the concept of privacy as non-disclosure. For example:

> Things that are only for me and I don't share them with anyone. (Ivana, 32, Spain)

> Things you keep to yourself, you don't want other people knowing about yourself. Like things you don't want the general public or your friends to know. Maybe close friends, but not the wider circle of friends. (Caroline, 26, UK)

As Caroline commented, sometimes people disclose what they consider their private information to a close circle of friends. Within these close circles of friends, confidentiality, built on trust, is implied, as the following quotes show:

> Privacy for me is just, I suppose, close to confidentiality, so whatever I say stays there. (Mateo, 43, UK)

> Something private is something I tell to people I trust that I know they are not going to talk about that to other people. (Gemma, 43, Spain)

In relation to confidentiality, some participants referred to control over personal information, and who has access to it, to define the concept of privacy. On the other hand, there were a few participants who also mentioned the notion of space to define privacy. In relation to personal space, Viel (38, Spain) claimed that cultural differences were key in creating misunderstandings around what was an acceptable behaviour when interacting with people from other cultures:

> I'm a touchy person. [...] It's something cultural different but if you are travelling this is something that cultural differences make people, like first impressions, reject you. For us (Spanish people), like to kiss to each other, it's something natural. (Viel, 38, Spain)

By the same token, Ivana (who is originally from Poland but lives in Spain) also thought that in Spain people are very touchy by her standards.

On the other hand, other participants defined privacy in relation to the concept of publicity, as opposed to publicity. Some of them also referred to that relationship as a continuum, as the following excerpt from an interview with John indicates:

> I think for me anything that is discernible from just my everyday public life. So the things I do out in public at the street: go out with my friends, be a white heterosexual male, all of those things I don't consider them private because I do them publicly. I think that the things that I'm concerned about are things that I do privately. So my sex life that's private, the fact that I'm straight and white is not. [...] So I guess it's about levels of privacy and there are some things, my name is entirely public, certainly my first name: entirely public, and my bank details: entirely private. Everything else sits on a spectrum [...] for how public or how private it is. (John, 28, UK)

In relation to the concept of privacy as opposite to publicity, some scholars (e.g., Garzón 2003) represent the interplay of publicity, privacy, and intimacy as concentric circles where intimacy would be in the centre, a realm that only the self can access; the private realm would be open to close relationships; the public realm would be open to everybody. Some participants referred to a similar concept and described intimacy as something personal to oneself. For instance, Raquel (35, Spain) explains that intimacy is something more inner than privacy: "Privacy is towards others, and intimacy is more something seen from me." Still, other participants included the significant other in the circle of intimacy as well. For instance, Caroline (26, UK) explains that what she shares with her partner is intimate, while what she shares with her friends would only be private. In relation to this, some participants located the concept of intimacy within privacy. For example:

> I would consider intimate to be the subsection of privacy that relates to personal details and to my personal life rather than my business or professional life. (John, 28, UK)

> Intimacy for me refers to how close you are with the partner. What you actually do with that partner. It's a very private word for me, it's, you know, what I do with my partner "behind closed doors". So for me intimacy is our sex, I miss you, stay, see you later, that's intimacy. (Oscar, 43, UK)

Oscar highlighted that for him intimacy was both physical and emotional, but it was always related to his partner. There were other participants who also related intimacy to the body and sexuality. Nevertheless, many participants explained that for them intimacy was not only sexual, but was also related to a feeling of closeness to another person, an emotional connection. Some participants also referred to reciprocity in the intimate connection between two people, to complicity, "because just with one sight we know what the other is thinking about" (Cesar, 44, Spain). On the other hand, one of the characteristics that most participants emphasized was that intimacy is exclusive: "for your eyes only", as the following interview extracts show:

So intimacy is more like close, you don't do that with everybody, with a selected people, closer number of people. (Mario, 36, UK)

So intimacy, you are going to share things to people you are close to, your close friends, your lovers or whatever. You don't share with all your friends, only with selected people. (Gary, 41, UK)

These circles of intimacy are created and sustained with an expectation of trust. Even some participants highlighted that it was trust first and then intimacy:

Intimacy is more for myself, or with a very small group of people that I really trust, that I know they are not going to tell someone else. (Gemma, 43, Spain)

Many participants had a real problem coming up with different definitions of privacy and intimacy. Some participants defined intimacy as their private life, which led them again to the concept of privacy. There were a number of participants who found it very difficult to distinguish between the two concepts. Despite the fact that some participants conceptualize intimacy as a euphemism for sex, the main conclusion I arrived at after analysing these interviews was that most participants located intimacy in the private realm. They identified privacy as the protection of intimacy, and most of them asserted that intimacy lost its status in cases where it was revealed in the "public gaze", like some scholars have highlighted (e.g., Sibilia 2008; Mateus 2010). After discussing with participants about their concepts of intimacy and privacy, I analysed how participants conceptualize privacy in social media interactions, focusing on the concepts of social and institutional privacy (Raynes-Goldie 2010), and how they deal with these affordances in order to experience privacy and intimacy when interacting through social media. Some participants expressed major concerns about social privacy (controlling access to personal information from peers) more than they expressed concerns about institutional privacy (how the platforms or governments use that information). In the next section, I explore how intimacy is understood in social media contexts and, in particular, whether participants believe the medium affects their understanding and practice of intimacy.

2.4   (Re)Defining Intimacy on Social Media

Increasingly people are using social media to create and maintain personal relationships. Social media appears as a new venue where intimacy practices are experienced and negotiated. For this reason, it is necessary to explore the concept of intimacy within these social media contexts to understand how it is transformed in "the process of mediation" (Silverstone 2005). In the age of social media, some authors (e.g., Giddens 1992; Papacharissi 2010; Rainie and Wellman 2012; Chambers 2013) argue, there is more freedom to choose intimate relationships outside of the family and the community, which has radically changed the way people interact. In this new social operating system, which Rainie and Wellman (2012) term *networked individualism* (2012, p. 3), they suggest that the individual becomes a *networked self*, "a single self that gets reconfigured in different situations as people reach out, connect, and emphasize different aspects of themselves" (2012, p. 126). This connects with Papacharissi's (2010) notion of the *networked self*, which emerges as a result of networked sociality afforded by social media.

In order to highlight the characteristics of intimacy through social media, most participants tended to compare online and offline settings. When comparing intimacy through social media and offline, there were diverse opinions about whether or not users could achieve intimacy online, and in the affirmative case, about whether there was more, less, or the same level of intimacy online than offline. Some participants claimed that it was not possible to experience intimacy on social media because of the publicity afforded by the medium, because they located intimacy within privacy. These participants were thinking only of interaction through public features, a topic that I will discuss further in the next section. Others considered it impossible to experience intimacy online, or they deemed online intimacy to be of lower quality than intimacy experienced face-to-face, because of the lack of physical interaction. On the other hand, some participants claimed that intimacy could be experienced through social media, though they identified some issues related to trust in the context of interaction with strangers.

Close/closer were words that some participants often used in order to describe intimacy in general, but interestingly participants did not mention these terms when talking about intimacy online. These definitions of intimacy were related more to physicality and embodiment. Following the previous definition of intimacy as *closeness*, in the context of social media interaction, there were a few participants who claimed that the feeling of closeness was related to the type of relationship, not to the means of communication:

> To me it doesn't really make any difference if it's online and not offline [...]. It doesn't really matter if you really connect to somebody, if it's on the other side of the world, if it's opposite you. [...] It doesn't matter if you do it through social media or whatever, it's the feel that you have for the person. (Mateo, 47, UK)

Later in the interview, Mateo specified that even though he believed that it is possible to experience intimacy interacting through social media, it is not the same level or quality of intimacy: "I think you can never substitute the real connection through human touch" (Mateo, 47, UK). However, in the case of the creation of new relationships, he considered that social media were a good starting point for developing intimacy in embodied encounters. Participants that considered it impossible or difficult to experience intimacy through social media had defined intimacy in relation to the body, particularly to sex. For this reason, they found that lack of physical contact would be an obstacle to experience intimacy:

> I guess you can have like webcam sex but that's not very intimate that's just wanking in front of a camera. I'd say that generally intimacy is better face-to-face and I don't think until they develop a really serious, clever computer plug-in that's always going to be the case, because intimacy is about physical, it's about looking in someone's eyes. If you wrote someone a love letter then, yes, of course Facebook is just as good as writing a letter although there's something more charming about a letter. That isn't the way that I

would be intimate with someone. I want to hold their hand or look into their eyes or be in bed with them. (John, 28, UK)

You can't really tell if someone's being serious in a conversation when you're chatting. I can put "lol" but I'm looking like at you (serious face) and saying "lol" and I'm not laughing out loud. So you don't really know what the reaction is when you're saying something intimate, when you're chatting and you say something that person you don't exactly know what the reaction is. I would prefer it to be face-to-face. I would not chat and say to someone ... At least I would like to hear their voice, if not by chat, at least listen to them so I know exactly what they feel, how they're reacting to it. (Isaac, 26, UK)

Even though Isaac claimed to prefer face-to-face communication to online communication, he was a very extensive social media user. He had more than 1000 friends on Facebook, and 920 pictures uploaded to his profile. Originally from India, Isaac explained that he recently moved to the UK, and he used to communicate with his family and friends on a daily basis through Facebook. Thus, we can observe that despite his preference for offline interaction, he was mainly communicating with his significant others through social media because it was the most convenient means of communication in his current personal situation as an expat.

The lack of physicality, which was deemed problematic for developing intimacy online, was considered positive for shy people in order to foster intimate self-disclosure. Some participants explained that they found it easier to communicate deeper thoughts and feelings through social media because they did not have to face their interlocutors:

I would say you can probably say more things online than you would say offline, face-to-face, just because you've got a kind of barrier there, so maybe you feel you are in your home environment, you feel more comfortable to say things there, meanwhile face-to-face I may not, you know, say something, I'd probably lie instead of like saying it, but online you probably could say it because you, you know, in front of the screen it's more ... easier, it's less fuss or something, so you can say whatever you want. (Caroline, 26, UK)

In Badoo people are more daring, if you are shy, for instance, because you don't have the person in front of you. (Petro, 29, Spain)

These participants found that social media act as intimacy facilitators, because it is easier for them to talk through digital means rather than face-to-face. Esteban, who is a high school teacher, observed that for many people "the Internet is a great help, they are all the time connecting and writing" (Esteban, 35, Spain). In this sense, participants linked intimacy on social media with self-disclosure. As Jamieson (2013, p. 18) points out, online self-disclosure "may generate a fleeting sense of intimacy between hitherto strangers or developing the intimacy of an already established relationship that began with co-presence". Thus, some participants when defining intimacy through social media identified the concept with self-disclosure:

> Personal experiences like just whatever you feel – whatever you feel comfortable putting on there like information or personal experiences, memories or like photographs. (Lulu, 25, UK)

> Sharing deeper personal information and photos. (David, 29, UK)

Gary, speaking about Badoo, related self-disclosure through the chat feature to reciprocity: "I generally say or disclose as much as it's disclosed back to me" (Gary, 41, UK). Also, other participants relate the concept of intimacy as *self-disclosure* to the notion of trust: they need to trust the other users in order to disclose intimate information to them, and at the same time, through the disclosure of personal and intimate information about themselves, they build trust in one another. In the context of the creation of new relationships, most participants considered it problematic to achieve closeness through digital communication because they have trust issues with the medium itself and with other users, a topic that will be discussed further in Chap. 6.

The previous discussion highlights the wide and diverse range of opinions that participants have regarding the topic of intimacy in social media. While some participants thought it was impossible or problematic to experience intimacy through social media because of the lack of physicality, and trust issues related to authenticating the information received, others considered that intimacy may be experienced, and even enhanced, through social media interaction, especially in the case of shy people. Therefore, in relation to whether intimacy on social media exists, is redefined, or is illusory, the findings suggest that it is possible to achieve intimacy when interacting through social media, although for some participants it would be of less quality since it is not possible to see or touch the other person to observe their reaction to your intimate self-disclosure. By the same token, some participants pointed out that the lack of physical cues causes mistrust about what people they meet on social media tell them, and this prevents intimacy to flourish, since for many participants the development of intimacy was based on trust. On the other hand, for other participants, intimacy would be enhanced online, since they found it easier to disclose intimate information through the screen. In general, we could conclude that intimacy through social media is mainly experienced as an emotional connection achieved through self-disclosure based on trust. The characteristic of mutuality, described by Zelizer's (2009) as inherent to intimacy, was seldom mentioned by participants when defining intimacy online. Although some participants referred to the chat feature when discussing online intimacy, most participants thought about intimacy on social media as intimacy through public features. In the next section, I discuss whether participants think that intimacy can be experienced through public features and whether they participate in these public intimacy practices.

2.5   From Diaries to Profiles: The Rise and Fall of Public Intimacy?

In contemporary society, Berlant (1997) argues, we are experiencing the ascendance of public intimacy, within what she labels the "affective turn". This intimate public sphere, Berlant (1997) suggests, arises as a result of the process of collapsing the political and the personal. In contemporary society, intimate lives are increasingly represented and articulated in public realms. Scholars also link this shift to the emergence of social media. As Hinton and Hjorth (2013) put it: "social media affords certain kinds of social performance that involve making intimacy more public" (2013, p. 3). Hinton and Hjorth (2013, p. 139) point to an "intimacy turn" on social media interaction, where affection is the glue of users' engagement with the platform. They use the term "intimate publics" (2013, p. 44) in order to talk about social media users in this context.

On the other hand, Taddicken and Jers (2011) argue that although intimacy may be established in social media through limited access, the sense of intimacy is usually illusive. Also, Van Manen (2010) suggests that "digital intimacy" can be illusory as a result of publicness of social media interaction. Sibilia (2008) and Mateus (2010) apply the Lacanian concept of *extimacy* (the public exhibition of intimacy) to the social web, while

David (2009) describes this phenomenon by using the term "exteriorized intimacy" (2009, p. 86). Sibilia (2008) suggests that social media are widely used to perform intimacy in public, thus intimacy ceases to be, becoming *extimacy*. The extreme case of *extimacy* is when people are eager to display intimate lives in public.

As stated by Jamieson (2012), sharing emotions and feelings with others has always been part of intimacy practices; the public nature and scope of these practices in the context of social media appear to contradict the secrecy and exclusiveness previously associated with the concept of intimacy in Western societies. Following this debate, David (2009, p. 86) questions the reasons why people may want to engage in this public exposure and how the very nature of intimacy may be transformed: "If we share our memories or our privacy, does our intimacy become public? Is privacy now public and intimacy that what privacy used to be?" This concept connects with Garzón's (2003) notion about when intimacy is disclosed, it is transferred to the private or even to the public realm. By the same token, David (2009, p. 84) suggests that the concepts of sharing and intimacy are intertwined online: "Previously iconic and sacred, intimacy is nowadays sometimes overexposed, and intertwines with the concept of sharing: we show and give ourselves to be seen by others." Mateus (2010) believes that the nature of intimacy is transformed in the process of becoming public, destroying secrecy, and installing a new concept. Nevertheless, Mateus (ibid.) believes that individuals make public only a small part of their inner thoughts and feelings.

Social media, according to boyd (2008, p. 19), make social information more easily accessible and "can rupture people's sense of public and private by altering the previously understood social norms". Nissenbaum (2009) argues that activities and interactions on social media cannot be clearly categorized as either public or private within this dichotomy. Jurgenson and Rey (2012) agree with boyd (2008) that privacy and publicity are "intertwined" and assert that "publicity and privacy do not always come at the expense of one another but, at times, can be mutually reinforcing" (2012, p. 191). For example, when someone shares part of a story publicly through social media, there is always a part of the story that is not told; hence, the rest of the story becomes more valuable for those who can access it, and the relationship with the confidant is made more intimate by giving them exclusive access. This connects with Reiman's (1976) idea that intimacy is a commodity valued by its scarcity.

While some scholars (e.g., Hogan 2010; Gürses and Díaz 2013; Young and Quan-Haase 2013) have demonstrated that users tend to share only superficial information on Facebook, in order to keep their social privacy, other scholars (e.g., Papacharissi and Gibson 2011; Turkle 2011; Jordán-Conde et al. 2013) argue that intimacy is increasingly performed in public through social media. They suggest that people have succumbed to the affordance of the networked life by choosing continual connectivity at the expense of privacy. In this view, more and more people are exposing their intimate lives through social media. This practice, which can be both empowering and risky, challenges the traditional concept that the development of intimacy requires privacy. These tensions highlight how the social media environment complicates the negotiation of privacy concerns with social and emotional desires to be accomplished within these networks. In order to explore public intimacy practices on social media, the first question that arises is whether participants consider social media to be public or private. Thus, in this section, I analyse how participants understand social media settings in relation to privacy/publicity. Then, I address the issue of public intimacy through social media. The main objective is to discuss whether participants engage in public intimacy practices, and examine their views about these practices.

Social media platforms provide both public and private means of interaction. Despite these private features, in general, participants considered social media to be public because of the publicity they afford, although a few participants reported that insofar as they had applied privacy settings to their social media profiles, they were private. For instance, Petro, a heavy social media user, contemplated that users can experience intimacy online insofar as it is protected by the privacy afforded by the configuration of the privacy settings, although he acknowledged that it is complicated because privacy settings policies change very often: "[Y]ou have to be careful because they are always changing the privacy policy, you always have to update which is available for the others and which is not" (Petro, 28, Spain). On the other hand, David, a UK-based participant, affirmed that the information published on social media is not entirely public or entirely private but "somewhere between the two" (David, 31, UK). Also, some other participants believed that social media could be either public or private depending on the nature of the information you post. In general, all participants agreed that social media was an open environment where privacy was hard to achieve. Most participants considered social media platforms to be public spaces, mainly in reference to the publicity they allow and because, despite applying privacy settings, on average they had a large number of friends (on Facebook). On the other hand, when asking participants if the information they publish on social media was public or private, most of them asserted that private information loses its status as private and its status as intimate when it is published through social media, as we can see in the following quote:

> I think that when you go online you enter in a realm that is not intimate… what could it be the most intimate? Maybe something I published on Facebook, something related to me, but as it goes out from my intimacy it becomes more, more of network. […] I decide what is not intimate anymore and goes to the social sphere. (Raquel, 35, Spain)

Yet, there were some participants who thought they could experience intimacy in public. In particular, one participant observed that people can see the intimacy in public but they cannot participate in it: "I think it can be shared between two people in a wider area, but it's only you two who are experiencing it" (Caroline, 26, UK). Nevertheless, most participants agreed that they did not negotiate their private lives through social media very often, for instance: "No, I'm not publishing anything connected with my private life" (Noelia, 25, UK). Examples of the few self-reported intimacy practices in public through social media can be seen in the following interview extracts:

> Viel (her partner) posted in Russian. I think that the day when I moved here and he posted a message; his Russian-speaking friend helped him. In Russian: "Now nobody is going to tear us apart" and I went: "Ohhhhh". […] I usually try not to participate in these kinds of conversations in public. […] It's only for two people because what I say sometimes in our friends list, though we are open to our friends, but there are random people and from time to time I have to check my friend list just to delete some people. (Vanessa, 29, Spain)

> I have had like nice conversations with people on Facebook, you know, like: "I love you, and I love you …". I think that the reason why you write it on the wall, instead of send them a message, is because you want other people to see it. But a lot of the time I just send messages as well, because I feel awkward people seeing stuff like that. I don't know, sometimes I put it on the wall. (Lulu, 25, UK)

In general, female participants seemed more concerned about people outside from their social circle watching them. Interestingly, although some male participants explained that they shared some intimate things on Facebook (a common statement was: "I have nothing to hide"). A popular topic about intimacy in public through social media was related to exhibitionism. As Thompson (2008) observes, some social media intimacy practices are connected with celebrity culture, and some people behave as celebrities, exposing their intimacy online in order to gather more likes and followers. John observed these kinds of practices and considered them egocentric. Following this discussion, Mario, in line with his definition of intimacy, stated that intimacy needed to be protected by privacy, that it is why he could not understand why people engage in public intimacy practices:

> It's a thing you experience with your wife, why do you have to share it with all the public? […] Why do you put that on Facebook? If you put that for me it's not intimate. You don't put things that are intimate, which are closer to you. So if you go to my profile and check my pictures, I don't think you'll see any of those, because with those I would have protected them, so if it's there anyone can see this. (Mario, 36, UK)

Mario related intimacy to the private realm. He suggested that intimacy needed the protection of privacy, as scholars such as Gerstein (1984) and Schoeman (1984) have also pointed out. Mario and other participants also questioned why people needed to exhibit their intimacy online. In this sense, some participants admitted that they used to post more often about their whereabouts, but they had diminished this practice notably in recent years:

> Some people (we) abuse a bit of the wall, we use it like our diary, where we write our intimate things. I have even used the Facebook wall to write very intimate things, and I'm now a bit more conservative in that sense. (Raquel, 35, Spain)

> I like less and less sharing my things, I don't share so many things, I don't care that much telling what I'm doing. There was this trend of having to tell what you were doing all the time, but I don't tell everything I do now. If I want to say something to someone I send them an email. (Gemma, 43, Spain)

This constant intimate self-disclosure through social media can generate *ambient intimacy* (Reichelt 2007), a term that defines the possibility to "keep in touch with people with a level of regularity and intimacy that you wouldn't usually have access to, because time and space conspire to make it impossible", or can produce, in some occasions, digital crowding (Joinson et al. 2011), which is the overexposure of personal information. Likewise, some participants expressed that they feel uncomfortable with these *extimacy* practices through social media and define them as "awkward". Most participants expressed their discomfort with these practices, finding them annoying and kind of intrusive. In particular, most participants agreed that sexual orientation, relationship status, sex, relationship problems, and overly emotional disclosures were not appropriate to be published on social media. I will discuss which topics participants considered intimate when interacting on social media and how they negotiated their publication in next chapter.

Since social media is considered mainly to be public, therefore we can say that intimacy on social media is usually intimacy in public, although for some participants, intimacy in public (through social media) is an oxymoron, as they identify intimacy as privacy. Most participants claimed that it was hard to achieve privacy on social media because of the number of friends they had on these platforms or due to the affordances of digital communication, yet some of them pointed to the use of private features or to the configuration of privacy settings as a way of communicating privately. In fact, most participants identified social media with their public features (e.g., the wall, the profile). A few participants saw themselves as having engaged in public intimacy practices through social media, but they explained that they tried to keep them to a minimum. A common statement was in reference to the frustration of having "too much" information about their friends' lives through Facebook, which highlights the characteristic of intimacy to be shared with(in) a small group of people: a group of significant others.

Most people do not want to be intimate with everybody; they find that annoying. By the same token, most participants do not post intimate information on Facebook, although some of them did not untag themselves from intimate pictures posted by partners (e.g., kissing). This implies that they accept that level of public intimate disclosure with their significant others, but they would not allow that kind of intimate disclosure with people outside of their intimate circle. It seems that most participants share a common understanding of what is appropriate to publish on

Facebook, which shows that social media practices shape users' behaviour and create non-written rules that help them to navigate their interaction through the platform.

2.6   CONCLUSIONS

In this study, the definition of emotional intimacy as a "sense of closeness within personal relationships, achieved by sharing inner thoughts and feelings" has been validated. Intimacy was often located within privacy and, as a result, some participants identified both concepts and considered it inappropriate to disclose intimacy in public, as it was often seen as an act of exhibitionism. Most participants' perceptions of privacy were in line with Schoeman's (1984) privacy definition, where privacy includes the norms which protect personal and intimate information and it is also the gated space where people can develop meaningful relationships away from the watch of the outsiders. In addition, most participants were more concerned about their social privacy than about their institutional privacy. The fact that participants' concerns are related to their social privacy highlights the importance of intimacy in their lives. In this sense, more policies to protect social privacy online should be implemented, or existing law, such as the privacy law, should be properly applied online, in cases of disclosure of intimate information by other users without permission, such as cases of revenge porn.

Most participants used the word "sharing" in order to describe the conveyance of information about the self through social media. The activity of sharing entails specific interpersonal dynamics, such as trust, reciprocity, and openness, which are the dynamics that most participants also identified within their intimacy practices on social media. There were a few participants who stated that the lack of embodiment made social media a bad tool with which to achieve intimacy. Conversely, some participants explained that they found it easier to communicate deeper thoughts and feelings through social media because they did not need to face their interlocutors, an argument that has been corroborated by numerous early studies of CMC (e.g., Walther 1996; Bargh and McKenna 2004). In this sense, they pointed out that social media is a good tool for shy people to develop personal relationships. In the context of the creation of new relationships, through self-disclosure, people develop a feeling of closeness with strangers that may be a good starting point to build a relationship offline. In the case of existing relationships, that feeling of closeness may be conveyed through the disclosure of shared memories through pictures, or keeping intimate conversation through the chat, but in general participants did not use public features (e.g., the wall, references) to be intimate with their contacts.

Despite social media platforms allowing users to configure privacy settings and providing private features to communicate, participants mainly considered social media to be a public venue in reference to the publicity these services afford. Some participants explained that they used to publish more intimate information in the past, but they had stopped revealing intimate information since they did not consider it appropriate to publish it anymore—most of them deemed this practice inappropriate and even disturbing. After an initial phase of experimentation with the use of social media, and the publicity they allow, it seems that participants have learned and internalized social norms that govern different social media platforms, wherein users generally do not reveal intimate information. Despite growing debates towards a more public disclosure of intimacy, in my study, participants preferred to communicate in private to negotiate intimate relationships or disclose intimate topics. In fact, most participants considered public intimacy to be anti-normative, since they considered that intimacy should remain in the private realm.

References

Bargh, J. A., & McKenna, K. Y. (2004). The Internet and social life. *Annual Review of Psychology, 55*(February), 573–590.

Berlant, L. G. (1997). *The queen of America goes to Washington city: Essays on sex and citizenship.* Durham, NC: Duke University Press.

Berlant, L. G. (2000). *Intimacy.* Chicago: University of Chicago Press.

Baym, N. K. (2010). *Personal connection in the digital age.* Cambridge: Polity Press.

boyd, d. (2008). Facebook's privacy trainwreck: Exposure, invasion, and social convergence. *Convergence, 14*(1), 13–20.

Chambers, D. (2013). *Social media and personal relationships: Online intimacies and networked friendship.* Basingstoke: Palgrave Macmillan.

David, G. (2009). Clarifying the mysteries of an exposed intimacy. In J. K. Nyíri (Ed.), *Engagement and exposure: Mobile communication and the ethics of social networking* (pp. 77–86). Viena: Passagen-Verlag.

Derlega, V. J., & Berg, J. H. (1987). *Self-disclosure: Theory, research, and therapy.* New York: Plenum Press.

Fried, C. (1968). Privacy: [A moral analysis]. In F. Schoeman (Ed.), *Philosophical dimensions of privacy: An anthology* (pp. 203–222). Cambridge: Cambridge University Press.

Garde-Hansen, J., & Gorton, K. (2013). *Emotion online: Theorizing affect on the internet.* New York: Palgrave Macmillan.

Garzón, E. (2003). Intimacy, privacy and publicity. *Analyse & Kritik, 25,* 17–40.

Gerstein, R. (1984). Intimacy and privacy. In F. Schoeman (Ed.), *Philosophical dimensions of privacy: An anthology* (pp. 265–271). Cambridge: Cambridge University Press.

Giddens, A. (1992). *The transformation of intimacy: Sexuality, love and eroticism in modern societies.* Cambridge: Polity Press.

Gürses, C., & Díaz, C. (2013). Two tales of privacy in online social networks. *Security & Privacy, 11*(3), 29–37.

Hinton, S., & Hjorth, L. (2013). *Understanding social media.* London: Sage Publications.

Hogan, B. (2010). The presentation of self in the age of social media: Distinguishing performances and exhibitions online. *Bulletin of Science, Technology & Society, 30*(6), 377–386.

Inness, J. C. (1996). *Privacy, intimacy, and solation.* Oxford: Oxford University Press.

Jamieson, L. (1998). *Intimacy: Personal relationships in modern societies.* Cambridge, MA: Polity Press.

Jamieson, L. (2012). Intimacy as a concept: Explaining social change in the context of globalisation or another form of ethnocentricism? *Sociological Research Online, 1*(1). http://clarion.ind.in/index.php/clarion/article/view/11. Date Accessed 9 Feb 2013.

Jamieson, L. (2013). Personal relationships, intimacy and the self in a mediated and global digital age. In K. Orton-Johnson & N. Prior (Eds.), *Digital sociology* (pp. 13–33). New York: Palgrave Macmillan.

Joinson, A. N., Houghton, D. J., Vasalou, A., & Marder, B. L. (2011). Digital crowding: Privacy, self-disclosure, and technology. In S. Trepte & L. Reinecke (Eds.), *Privacy online: Perspectives on privacy and self-disclosure in the social web* (pp. 33–45). Heidelberg: Springer.

Jordán-Conde, Z., Mennecke, B., & Townsend, A. (2013). Late adolescent identity definition and intimate disclosure on Facebook. *Computers in Human Behavior, 33,* 356–366.

Jurgenson, N., & Rey, P. J. (2012). Comments on Sarah Ford's "Reconceptualization of privacy and publicity". *Information, Communication & Society, 15*(2), 287–293.

Lambert, A. (2013). *Intimacy and friendship on Facebook.* Basingstoke: Palgrave Macmillan.

Marar, Z. (2012). *Intimacy.* London: Routledge.

Mateus, S. (2010). Public intimacy. In *Sphera Publica: Revista de Ciencias Sociales y de la Comunicación* (Vol. 10, pp. 57–70).

Morgan, D. (2011). *Rethinking family practices.* Basingstoke: Palgrave Macmillan.

Nissenbaum, H. (2009). *Privacy in context: Technology, policy, and the integrity of social life.* Stanford: University Press.

Oxford English Dictionary. (2015). *Intimacy.* [Online]. Available from: http://www.oed.com/view/Entry/98503?redirectedFrom=intimacy#eid. Accessed 7 Jan 2014.

Papacharissi, Z. (2010). Conclusion: A networked self. In Z. Papacharissi (Ed.), *A networked self: Identity, community, and culture on social network sites.* London: Routledge.

Papacharissi, Z., & Gibson, P. L. (2011). Fifteen minutes of privacy: Privacy, sociability and publicity on social networks sites. In S. Trepte & L. Reinecke (Eds.), *Privacy online: Perspective on privacy and self-disclosure on the social web* (pp. 75–89). New York: Springer.

Plummer, K. (2003). *Intimate citizenship: Private decisions and public dialogues.* Seattle: University of Washington Press.

Rainie, H., & Wellman, B. (2012). *Networked: The new social operating system.* Cambridge, MA: MIT Press.

Raynes-Goldie, K. (2010). Aliases, creeping, and wall cleaning: Understanding privacy in the age of Facebook. *First Monday* [Online], *15*(1). Available from: http://firstmonday.org/article/view/2775/2432. Accessed 10 June 2014.

Reichelt, L. (2007, March 1). 'Ambient intimacy'. Disambiguity. http://www.disambiguity.com/ambient-intimacy/. Accessed 10 Dec 2016.

Reiman, J. (1976). Privacy, intimacy and personhood. *Philosophical and Public Affairs, 6*(1), 26–44.

Reis, H. T., & Shaver, P. (1988). Intimacy as an interpersonal process. In S. Duck (Ed.), *Handbook of personal relationships: Theory, research, and interventions* (pp. 367–389). Oxford: John Wiley & Sons.

Schoeman, F. (1984). Privacy and intimate information. In F. Schoeman (Ed.), *Philosophical dimensions of privacy: An anthology* (pp. 1–33). Cambridge, MA: Cambridge University Press.

Shaffer, D. R., & Tomarelli, M. M. (1989). When public and private self-foci clash: Self-consciousness and self-disclosure reciprocity during the acquaintance process. *Journal of Personality and Social Psychology, 56*(5), 765–776.

Sibilia, P. (2008). *La intimidad como espectáculo.* Buenos Aires: Fondo de Cultura Económica.

Silverstone, R. (2005). The sociology of mediation and communication. In C. Calhoun, C. Rojeck, & B. Turner (Eds.), *The SAGE handbook of sociology* (pp. 188–207). London: Sage.

Taddicken, M., & Jers, C. (2011). The uses of privacy online: Trading a loss of privacy for social web gratifications? In S. Trepte & L. Reinecke (Eds.), *Privacy online: Perspective on privacy and self-disclosure on the social web* (pp. 143–158). New York: Springer.

Thompson, C. (2008, September 15). Brave new world of digital intimacy. *New York Times Magazine* [Online]. Available from: http://www.nytimes.com/2008/09/07/magazine/07awareness-t.html. Accessed 5 June 2012.

Turkle, S. (2011). *Alone together: Why we expect more from technology and less from each other*. New York: Basic Books.

Van Manen, M. (2010). The pedagogy of momus technologies: Facebook, privacy, and online intimacy. *Qualitative Health Research, 20*(8), 1023–1032.

Walther, J. B. (1996). Computer-mediated communication impersonal, interpersonal, and hyperpersonal interaction. *Communication Research, 23*(1), 3–43.

Young, A. L., & Quan-Haase, A. (2013). Privacy protection strategies on Facebook: The Internet privacy paradox revisited. *Information, Communication & Society, 16*(4), 479–500.

Zelizer, V. A. (2009). *The purchase of intimacy*. Princeton: Princeton University Press.

CHAPTER 3

Intimacies of Digital Identity

Abstract The main objective of this chapter is to conduct a cross-platform analysis and identify disclosure patterns in three different social media platforms: Badoo, CouchSurfing, and Facebook. Drawing on Hogan's (2010) exhibitionistic approach, in this chapter, user profiles are analysed as cultural artefacts, which are tools for self-(re)presentation and impression management. The observation of user profiles is combined with the interviews with participants where they explained which topics they disclosed online and considered intimate. After a definition of the concepts of self-disclosure and self-(re)presentation, the topics that participants frequently identified as intimate when interacting through social media (relationship status, sexual orientation, political and religious beliefs, sex, alcohol intake, and feelings) are discussed in depth.

Keywords Badoo • CouchSurfing • Facebook • Intimate information • Online identity • Social media

3.1 INTRODUCTION

The creation of a profile is the first step in order to participate in social media services, as some authors (e.g., Baym 2010; Thumim 2012) observe, and usually implies the disclosure of certain kinds of information: name, gender, age, sexual orientation, relationship status, and so on,

© The Author(s) 2018
C. Miguel, *Personal Relationships and Intimacy in the Age of Social Media*, https://doi.org/10.1007/978-3-030-02062-0_3

amongst others. Thumim (2012) suggests that social media profiles are crafted representations. Social media platforms usually provide a closed number of categories to fill in, to represent the user in the network. Apart from fixed categories that users have to fill in, social media profiles have other sections where users can write more freely, for example, "About Me" section on Badoo and CouchSurfing, or "the wall" on Facebook. In these sections people discuss intimate topics such as political and religious beliefs, feelings, or sex. Nissenbaum (2009) explains that there are certain kinds of information related to the self that people expect to keep private, which are called intimacies of personal identity. Nissenbaum (2009, p. 123) states that intimacies of personal identity may include: "close relationships, sexual orientation, alcohol intake, dietary habits, ethnic origin, political beliefs, features of the body and bodily functions, the definitions of *self*, and religious and spiritual beliefs and practices". In this chapter, I analyse which topics participants considered more intimate when crafting their profile or interacting online, which, at the same time, inform debates about the relationship between privacy and intimacy. For example, when I talk about which topics participants considered intimate and which ones they disclosed in each social media platform, sometimes these topics are connected to participants' definitions of online intimacy and how they negotiate the disclosure of intimate information in different platforms. Beforehand, I consider it interesting to discuss the topics on self-presentation and self-disclosure in the next section.

3.2   ONLINE SELVES

In this section, I explore the role of online self-disclosure in developing intimate relationships. I also pay attention to the concept of self-(re)presentation, since it is a more curated type of self-disclosure. The concept of self-(re)presentation involves debates about performance, impression management, and authenticity. The following discussion suggests that both self-disclosure and self-(re)presentation foster the development of intimacy online. Self-disclosure does not need to be intimate, as playful or everyday information may also lead to the development of intimacy among social media users. In addition, curated self-(re)presentation, although it may be perceived as performance, which lacks authenticity, can help to claim attention from other users and, therefore, facilitate liking and intimacy.

3.2.1   Self-Disclosure

According to Archer and Burleson (1980), self-disclosure consists of revealing personal information to other people. Some authors (e.g., Reis and Shaver 1988; Joinson et al. 2011) link the quantity and depth of self-disclosure with the development of intimacy. As Joinson and others (2011) put it: "[B]y controlling disclosure, individuals manage the degree of intimacy in a relationship" (2011, p. 36). Self-disclosure can be analysed in three dimensions: frequency, breath, and depth, as Nguyen et al. (2012, p. 103) observe, where the depth dimension would be defined as the "intimacy of personal information divulged". Intimate self-disclosures contain valuable information related to thoughts and feelings, which help others to get to know the person better. This is the basis of the social penetration theory formulated by Altman and Taylor (1973), which also suggests that self-disclosure helps to improve understanding and liking.

The breadth and depth of the information shared increase as the relationship develops. Altman and Taylor (1973) observed that as relationships progress, individuals start to share more and deeper intimate information. Nevertheless, Utz (2015) argues that social penetration theory is not enough to explain relationship development on social media where most public posts are not intimate, but include humour and are entertaining. In her research about self-disclosure through social media among German students, she found that in the context of social media interaction, social penetration theory was validated in private communication, but, at the same time, public entertaining self-disclosures also helped to create a feeling of connection. Her participants engaged much more in private communication when they wanted to discuss intimate topics. Similarly, Lambert (2013, p. 177) identifies "playfulness" as a characteristic of public communication among intimates. He (2013, p. 172) argues that despite the inexistence of deep emotions in this type of "fun" communication, it is a signal of "warmth of an interpersonal bond".

As we saw earlier, intimacy involves some kind of love, liking, or caring. In their recent research Sprecher and colleagues (2013) found that the recipient of disclosure experiences more liking and closeness than the discloser. Similarly, Utz (2015) discovered that people like the ones to whom they self-disclose, but not necessarily the ones who disclose intimate information to them. In this regard, some scholars (e.g., Thompson 2008; Hjorth et al. 2012) affirm that continuous awareness through textual and visual self-disclosure, constantly knowing banal information about people you know (i.e. what your friends had for breakfast), may create what Reichelt (2007) calls *ambient intimacy*. However, since too much self-disclosure may lead to reduced liking, Joinson et al. (2011) suggest that overexposure in the context of social media may produce *digital crowding*, a term that means excessive social contact or insufficient personal space, which may affect personal relationships.

Thus, users have to find a balance between enough self-disclosure to develop intimacy and too much disclosure, which would lead to rejection. There are also social norms about what it is acceptable to disclose or not at different stages of the development of a relationship and in relation to the kind of relationships kept with others, as Joinson et al. (2011, p. 36) put it: "It is not just the environment that dictates social norms and expectancies of self-disclosure, but also the nature of the relationship between interaction partners." Similarly, Cohen (2012) states that in the context of social media, self-presentation management skills are used to handle different kinds of relationships.

Drawing on the enhanced self-disclosure theory, Jiang and Hancock (2013) analysed self-disclosure as an intimacy-enhancing process across different interpersonal media. Jiang and Hancock (2013) suggest that the affordances of each medium would influence the development of intimacy. Early CMC research (e.g., Walther 1996; Bargh and McKenna 2004) showed that text-based communication enhanced self-disclosure, and intimacy as a result. Walther (1996) developed the hyperpersonal communication theory, which states that online communication is more socially desirable than face-to-face communication because it allows strategically selecting, editing, and improving self-presentation. It is suggested that the control over their self-disclosure and the lack of physical cues may make users feel more comfortable to disclose intimate information, which may generate stronger intimacy. Walther (1996) also found that users who engage in CMC tend to idealize to their counterparts. Following Walther, Qiu et al. (2012) suggest that users tend to publish positive emotions to improve their social image. Likewise, Illouz (2007), in her research about dating sites, recognizes this ideal that the self is better expressed online without the constrictions of the body, but concludes that it is not that the Internet enhances intimacy, but it allows people to connect and increases sociability and relationships. In addition, early Internet research (e.g., Walther 1996; Bargh and McKenna 2004) suggested that the anonymity facilitated by chat rooms and bulletin boards (which usually did not include pictures) fostered self-disclosure and helped to build intimate relationships. In the same vein, Lasén (2013) observes that users tend to disclose more intimate information online because they feel less embarrassment. Nevertheless, Walther and Parks (2002) concluded that people considered CMC less intimate than face-to-face interaction. Nguyen et al. (2012) reviewed the literature in this area, concluding that self-disclosure was not found to be greater online than face-to-face. In a study about Facebook, Park et al. (2011) found out that self-disclosure online does lead to the development of intimacy, just as in face-to-face interaction. However, they argue that users' awareness of the curated self-(re)presentation on the site may hinder the transformation into intimacy.

3.2.2   Self-(Re)Presentation

In the process of creating a social media profile, scholars (e.g., Baym 2010; Joinson et al. 2011; Thumim 2012) emphasize that self-(re)presentation and the disclosure of certain kinds of information (location, name, gender, sexual orientation, etc.) are preconditions for participation in social media service. On social media profiles self-(re)presentation is both textual and visual. Most profiles provide a section including a user's personal description and what things the user likes, which is usually called the "About Me" section. Baym (2010, p. 110) explains that social media platforms foster users to disclose interests and tastes in order to find like-minded people: "the assumption being that people who share tastes are likely to be interpersonally compatible and hence good prospects for relational success". Illouz (2007) looked at 100 "About Me" sections and found that most people used the same kind of adjectives to describe themselves (e.g. "I am fun and adventurous"). Illouz (ibid.) suggests that self-descriptions are led by cultural scripts of desirable personality. The crafting of the profile, argues Illouz (2007), implies a process of self-reflection. Similarly, Miller (2011, p. 179) points out that this process may lead to self-knowledge: "Facebook is a virtual place where you discover who you are by seeing a visible objectification of yourself." Following this, Lambert (2013, p. 40) suggests that Facebook functions as a mirror where people can observe and analyse their own behaviours, which can contribute to "a kind of media self-awareness".

The representation of the self on social media is also curated in order to manage personal relationships. Several scholars (e.g., Baym 2010; Hogan 2010; Brake 2014) have applied the dramaturgical framework developed by Goffman (1969) to analyse how users engage in impression management through social media. Goffman (ibid.) developed the concept of "drama", which emphasizes the fact that all people interpret roles in the "drama" of everyday life. For Goffman, interpersonal lives are marked by performance, and life unfolds as a "drama". Individuals try to manage the ways that others perceive them, and try to present themselves in a positive way. Hence, social media platforms are seen as the new stages where the "drama" can be also performed. Thumim (2012) distinguishes between "self-presentation" or performance, that we continuously engage in, which is often an unconscious process, and "self-representation", which is a conscious and curated representation of the self, that we can find (among other places) on social media. If we do not engage in impression management to address different audiences or we gather all these audiences in the same setting, *context collapse* (e.g., Ellison et al. 2011; Marwick and boyd 2011) may occur. Ellison et al. (2011, p. 30) observe that access to novel information on Facebook may help to bridge social capital, but "it may also result in negative personal or professional outcomes associated with the unanticipated disclosure of information about the self to unintended audiences". Therefore, they identify potential privacy risks involved in self-disclosure to unintended audiences in the context of social media.

In relation to textual disclosures, Jordán-Conde et al. (2013) ranked three "highly intimate" topics, including: death, sex, and emotions. On the other hand, Lomborg (2013) found out that information about spouses and children was deemed appropriate and occasionally shared by Twitter users, while relationship problems and sex lives were considered to be too intimate and rarely tweeted about. Likewise, Pedroni et al. (2014) discovered that posts with excessive expression of feelings (aka "deep intimacy"), or with references to sex, were not considered appropriate by Facebook users. In the next section I will focus the attention on sexual orientation and relationship status to highlight the important role that disclosing these types of information plays in social media interaction.

3.3   SEXUAL ORIENTATION AND RELATIONSHIP STATUS

Sexual orientation and relationship status are closely interrelated topics. In the case of having a partner, the disclosure of his or her identity through social media may imply sexual orientation, although obviously it does not show the full sexual identity of the user. Half of the participants disclosed their sexual orientation on Badoo, Facebook, or CouchSurfing. Some participants considered sexual orientation as an intimate topic, and few of them still disclosed this information online, mainly on Badoo. All Badoo participants disclosed their sexual orientation on Badoo, although none of them disclosed it on Facebook. In fact, few other participants disclosed their sexual orientation through Facebook. Some Badoo users explained that on Badoo, it was necessary to specify their sexual orientation because the platform was designed for those looking for a romantic or sexual partner, but they did not find it necessary to disclose that information on Facebook. Patricia, a 31-year-old Spain-based Badoo user, defined herself as a lesbian, and she actually considered sexual orientation an intimate topic. She explained that for her, it was easier to disclose her sexual orientation through social media than face-to-face. As we saw in the previous chapter, some participants, like Patricia, found it easier to disclose intimate information online than face-to-face because they felt somehow protected by the screen. In relation to the disclosure of her sexual orientation, Patricia highlighted that disclosing that she was gay on Badoo was paramount because she was looking for a partner and she needed to show her preferences to avoid male users contacting her. The rest of the Badoo participants claimed to be straight. Nevertheless, Sandra (39, UK), who disclosed through her Badoo profile that she was straight and had children, explained during the interview that she was bi-curious[1] and that she started to chat with other women on the site until she finally found a female partner. Thus, in my research, most LGBT participants expressed their concern about disclosing their sexual orientation on Facebook, and one of them even lied about this topic in this platform. Viel (38, Spain), who considered sexual orientation as being intimate, was actually in a straight relationship, and appeared on Facebook as interested in women. Nevertheless, he explained during the interview that he was bisexual but that his girlfriend did not feel comfortable with his sexual orientation. That may be the reason why he wanted to emphasize through his Facebook profile that he was straight, in order to make his girlfriend feel more comfortable.

Caroline (26, UK), a lesbian participant who did not identify sexual orientation as an intimate topic in the first place, clarified during the inter-

---

[1] Bi-curious: (Of a heterosexual person) interested in having a sexual experience with a person of the same sex (*Oxford English Dictionary*, 2018a).

view that she did not want to disclose it publicly through Facebook because she was "friends" with some family members who did not know she was a lesbian and she did not want them to know. Interestingly, although she did not indicate anything in the "Interested in" field, she liked several gay Facebook pages, which could be interpreted to convey her sexual orientation. Therefore, her actions did not correspond with her concerns about not revealing her sexual orientation. In this case, Caroline was engaging in self-presentation through her group membership. The expression of identity through self-disclosure, affiliation, and the interaction with other users has been labelled "mosaic identity" (Lara 2007). In a second view of her profile, I observed that she was no longer a member of these lesbian Facebook groups. This management of her self-presentation to avoid the disclosure of too intimate information shows how users carefully curate their online presence in order to protect their intimacy. Caroline still disclosed her sexual orientation on CouchSurfing through her membership on lesbian groups. Since the interaction on CouchSurfing was with strangers, she did not find it problematic to disclose her sexual orientation on this platform.

Several participants actually disclosed their relationship status in one or more social media platforms. Relationship status was identified as an intimate topic by some participants, and half of them still disclosed their relationship status on Badoo, CouchSurfing, or Facebook. Raquel, the only Badoo user who specified that relationship status was intimate, during the course of the interview, clarified that she considered relationship status to be private instead of intimate, and she would not disclose that on a CV, for instance. She explained how she was asked in a job interview about it and she thought that the employer did not have the right to ask her about those kinds of private matters. Thus, taking into account Raquel's clarification, we could say that all Badoo participants disclosed their relationships status on Badoo, and none of them considered it to be intimate. It is possible that the use of a dating site and having to disclose this kind of information in order to participate on the service led them to think about this topic as not being intimate.

Due to the dating nature of Badoo, it is not surprising that all participants displayed their relationship status on the site as single. Two of them, who also facilitated their Facebook profile for the study, indicated that they were single on Facebook as well. Nevertheless, Robert (43, UK), who was actually in a relationship at the time of the interview, appeared as single in both his Badoo and his Facebook profiles. When I asked him why he appeared as single, given that he was in a relationship (he even received a phone call from his girlfriend in the course of the interview), he responded that he was not on good terms with his partner and he was looking for someone else. As with other participants, Robert deleted his relationships status from his Facebook profile later on. The trend of revealing only superficial information on Facebook in order to avoid context collapse, advanced by Hogan (2010), may be the reason why Robert and other users decided to delete this information. Sandra (39, UK) was in a relationship with another woman she met on Badoo; however, she appeared as single on the site. Hence, the fact that all participants appear as single on Badoo did not mean that they were actually single.

On CouchSurfing there is no field to specify relationship status; nevertheless, some participants, in the section "Couch Information", explained that they lived with their partners[2]. For instance, Vanessa (29, Spain), who actually met her boyfriend through CouchSurfing, considered her relationship status to be intimate, but pointed out that she felt the need to specify it on CouchSurfing because potential guests needed to know that they would be hosted by both Vanessa and her partner. She spoke in plural in most part of her CouchSurfing profile, describing the interests of both partners. Her boyfriend, Viel (38, Spain), also explained in his CouchSurfing profile that he was in a relationship with Vanessa and he even included a link to her profile. In the case of Facebook, Viel explained how they negotiated to publish their relationships status on social media, as she was reluctant to do it in the first place. This a good example of the tensions generated by different concepts of privacy and intimacy of partners in a relationship, and the complex negotiation of the exhibition of the happiness of the relationship versus the desire of privacy. At same point after the interview they both removed their relationship status from their Facebook profiles, although they still specified that they were a couple through their CouchSurfing profiles. The deletion of their relationship status on Facebook shows the tensions inherent in finding a balance between the different opinions partners may have about what is desirable to disclose on a particular social media platform regarding its publics. Thus, Vanessa considered it necessary to inform their potential CouchSurfing guests that Viel and she lived together, but she considered it intrusive for all of their

---

[2] It is also common practice for couples who live together to create a common CouchSurfing profile because they are both actually hosting other members.

Facebook friends to know about their relationship. In fact, most participants did not disclose their relationship status on Facebook. John (28,
UK), who did not consider relationship status as being intimate, but who
did not disclose it through Facebook, pointed out that the main reason he
did not want to disclose his relationships status was because of the moment
of the break-up, which he considered private. Thus, John acknowledged
that the real reason he was disturbed with the publicity of his relationship
status was related to the unwanted publicity of the potential end of the
relationship, which he wanted to keep private.

It is suggested that each type of social media platform has different
social norms. Sexual orientation and relationship status are the kinds of
information that are necessary and expected to be disclosed on Badoo
because the objective of using the site is to find a partner. Nevertheless, on
Facebook, most participants decided not to disclose this information in
order to avoid gossip about their private life. Especially LGBT participants
were more concerned about the disclosure of sexual orientation and
explicit information (e.g. pictures) showing their relationship status on
Facebook because of the possibility of reaching unintended audiences. In
the case of CouchSurfing, where the interaction was among strangers,
only Caroline (26, UK) could actually be identified as a lesbian because of
her membership in the CouchSurfing Lesbian group. In general, sexual
orientation was not considered as relevant information to be disclosed on
the CouchSurfing platform. Caroline pointed out that she joined the
CouchSurfing Lesbian group because she felt more comfortable exchanging hospitality within the LGBT community. On the other hand, in relation to relationship status, CouchSurfing participants who were living
with their partners considered it important to specify it because both of
them would host potential guests. Thus, a participant's decision to disclose sexual orientation and relationship status in the different social media
platforms was mainly led by what was needed or sociably desirable on each
platform rather than by their consideration of these topics as being intimate or not.

3.4   Religion and Political Views

Political and religious beliefs are fields that users can fill in when creating
a Facebook profile, although they are more usually expressed through
posts on the platform. Most participants did not disclose their political or
religious beliefs. There were only a few participants who actually filled out

the relevant fields on Facebook, and a few participants also joked in order not to disclose their real thoughts. Nevertheless, another way of conveying religious or political beliefs was through pictures, like in the case of Gemma, a 43-year-old Spain-based participant, who did not actually specify her political beliefs on the "Information" section, but was pictured holding an independence Catalonian flag in some of her pictures on Facebook. In the context of Badoo interaction, participants did not disclose any kind of religious or political beliefs. Some participants claimed that political and religious beliefs were intimate topics. When discussing the topic of religion, few participants considered it intimate. Among those, some users such as Luis (30, Spain), a Badoo and Facebook user, considered religion an intimate topic and explained how he would never post about the topic on social media.

On the other hand, there were other users who specified that religion was an intimate topic but they still disclosed it through their Facebook profile. Also, some participants changed their mind in relation to this topic during the course of the interview. For example, Mario, a UK-based CouchSurfing and Facebook user, first specified religion as an intimate topic through the pre-info sheet, but during the interview, he commented that he thought religion was more private than intimate. Other contradictions were appreciated in some participant's claim where she first said that she rarely tells anyone about her religious beliefs, and then she publishes that on Facebook. These kinds of contradictions demonstrate the complex task of defining what is intimate and what is not, and how to negotiate the disclosure of intimate information on social media. For some participants, expressing their religious beliefs on social media is not socially acceptable, while others felt comfortable publishing their religion online, although they did not often discuss the topic because they considered it too intimate (as Patricia explained in the case of her sexual orientation). Others did not have a clear idea whether religion was intimate or private, which is an ontological discussion that was presented in Chap. 2.

When discussing political beliefs during the interviews with participants who considered the topic intimate, I found different reasons why they considered this topic intimate and how they negotiated its disclosure or not through social media platforms. In the case of CouchSurfing, Viel (38, Spain) pointed out that the intimate information he disclosed through his CouchSurfing profile was actually his Catalan independence political beliefs, and he dedicated a lot of space in his profile to talk about the topic. In his CouchSurfing profile he described, among other data, that his first language was Catalonian, that he is an active member of a group of *castell-ers* (traditional human towers which are usually built in Catalonian celebrations), and why he considered Catalonia not to be part of Spain. For Viel, his political views were intimate, but they were an important part of his identity, and therefore he wanted to display them in public and so he dedicated a lot of space in his CouchSurfing profile to explain to potential guests facts about his Catalan identity and particularities of Catalonia.

On the other side of the spectrum we have John (28, UK), who did not disclose his political affiliation at all. John explained that because he was a journalist, he was supposed to be objective and he could not publicly declare his political beliefs. On the other hand, Mateo (47, UK), who did not disclose his political beliefs through any platform, described how he did not want to be associated with any radical political view through social media. Mateo, who was originally from Greece, commented that he even deleted "friends" from his Facebook profile if they were too politically radical because he was a pacifist and considered that these kinds of radicalisms were responsible for creating polarization in society. Walther et al. (2008) found in their research about impression management on Facebook that the appearance and behaviour of a user's friends played an important role in user's identity perception by other users in the network. Mateo seemed to be aware of this fact and also actively engaged in impression management to protect his image by unfriending extremist political contacts from his friend's list, in order not to be associated with them. Thus, among participants who classified political beliefs as intimate, there were three different approaches: (1) explicit disclosures on social media about their political views, (2) not to disclose any kind of political information, and (3) delete politically radical contacts in order not to be associated with them.

Finally, some participants did not have a clear idea about whether to classify political beliefs as intimate or not. For example, Lulu (25, UK), who did not disclose her political affiliation, affirmed that she usually posted about politics on Facebook. Although she did not indicate political beliefs as an intimate issue in the pre-info sheet, during the interview she described that she felt that posting about political beliefs was kind of intimate for her because it showed what she thought about a particular issue:

> I like talking about – I really like politics and I always post quite a lot of politics especially on Facebook, like I'll read an article and then I'll repost it and just like say a little thing about what I think. I guess that is like intimate in a way because that's how I feel about something but to me that's okay because

it's – why is that okay? I don't know, because it's not about something that's like sexual or about. (Lulu, 25, UK)

For Lulu, her political beliefs were an intimate topic, but she considered it acceptable to talk about them in public through social media. She suggested that it was socially acceptable to discuss politics in public (although for her it was a bit intimate) unlike sex, which was kind of taboo. In fact, explicit sexual references through social media profiles are still unusual. The negotiation of the representation of sexual behaviour and alcohol intake (which was also usually considered somewhat taboo) will be addressed in the next section.

3.5   Sex, Alcohol, and Social Media

Explicit sexual references and portraits of users being drunk in their own profiles are still taboo topics due to the potential damage of their reputation, especially when looking for a job. Sexual behaviour and alcohol intake were practices linked to parties, which could be observed in some young social media user profiles. Mendelson and Papacharissi (2010) identified a correlation between pictures of parties, where alcohol was present, and affectionate pictures (e.g., hugging or kissing on the lips) in Facebook photo albums. Nevertheless, in their research about Facebook photo galleries among college students, Mendelson and Papacharissi (ibid.) found that explicit sexual disclosure, and even posting pictures of people kissing on the lips, was rare to find in pictures uploaded to Facebook. Similarly, in my research, which is among adults (25–50 years old), explicit references to sex on participants' profiles were also uncommon. Only some participants had sexualized pictures in their profiles, either in a bikini or in revealing clothes.

As we saw in Chap. 2, the term intimacy is often used as a euphemism to mean sexual intercourse. In fact, when participants were asked to define their own concept of intimacy, some of them related the term exclusively to sex. The following quotes are some examples of participants linking both concepts. Participants often either choose not to disclose that kind of information or talked about sexual matters through the chat:

I don't know really, bedroom stuff? […] It depends who is with really but, say, if it's your girlfriend I wouldn't want to post information about when

I've had sex with her. So that would be really intimate in that relationship. (Isaac, 26, UK)

On Badoo for sure, talking about sex, talking about intimate things. (Viel, 38, Spain)

CouchSurfing was not mentioned in relation to sexual disclosure. Some participants commented on sexy pictures, especially on Badoo, as it is a dating/hook-up site, where users try to claim attention in different ways, and the use of erotic pictures is a common practice. Nevertheless, most participants did not include these kinds of pictures in their own profiles. In this sense, Luis (30, Spain) described the process of creating his Badoo profile. First, he uploaded some pictures, and then he checked other users' profiles and felt that he did not fit in the network because his pictures were not sexy:

I felt I was not using the same codes than the rest of the users. I felt a bit out of place. I was looking at profiles and I saw very sexy pictures, like club dancers, and pictures in the toilet and things like that … so I felt a bit out of place. (Luis, 30, Spain)

I will discuss the topic of sexy pictures on Badoo further, in particular in relation to gendered double standards, in Chap. 6. Although most Badoo participants made references to other users' profiles that included erotic pictures, most of the pictures in a bikini or half-naked were found on Facebook. I argue that the reason for having more sexy pictures on Facebook than on a dating site is because of the higher number of pictures that are actually available on Facebook. There were some female participants who explained they would not upload revealing pictures, for example, in a bikini, on Facebook. However, a few male participants who had several pictures in bathing suits on Facebook did not consider that intimate or problematic. Although male participants linked online intimacy with sex more often than female participants, in general, across all platforms, both male and female participants usually restricted conversations about sex to the chat and rarely uploaded sexy pictures.

Alcohol intake was another topic identified as intimate by participants. Alcohol intake was often disclosed through pictures, although on Badoo alcohol intake is also a category in the profile. It is possible to choose among: "No", "No, never", "In company" (previously called "Socially"), and "Yes, please". All Badoo participants filled in the field and none of them indicated that alcohol intake was an intimate topic. CouchSurfing was not a site that participants referred to when talking about the representation of parties and alcohol intake during the interviews. Nevertheless, Ivana (32, Spain), who indicated that alcohol intake was intimate, explained in several places in her CouchSurfing profile that she liked beer and wine, to emphasize that she drank alcohol on a regular basis. Then, the main question was how participants negotiate the disclosure of their drinking habits through Facebook.

Participants narrated that they usually untag themselves from pictures where they appeared clearly drunk, and that sometimes they even ask the person who uploaded the pictures or the platform itself to remove those pictures. Some participants claimed that alcohol intake was intimate, and half of these participants, in spite of this, had a lot of pictures on Facebook drinking, playing drinking games, and partying visibly drunk—more than the rest of participants who did not consider alcohol intake an intimate topic. For instance, Ivana (32, Spain) had some posts on her Facebook wall about being hung over, and some pictures of her partying with a lot of drinks around. Similarly, Mario (36, UK), who categorized alcohol intake as intimate, had a lot of pictures of him drinking on Facebook. Mario was one of the few participants who considered that if his profile was set to private, that information is private, although he contradicted himself later on when he said it was not possible to control intimacy on social media "because your friends can almost see everything you do." This participant might consider that the information he shared on his Facebook profile would remain in his personal circle, although he already considered this problematic, and because he had configured privacy settings, that information was supposed to be private. Another UK-based participant, John (28), who first stated that alcohol intake was intimate, changed his mind during the course of the interview and explained that he did not consider this topic intimate, and he did not feel embarrassed by people knowing that he drank in the evenings because he did it in public (implying that if it were intimate he would do it in private). I hypothesize that it was precisely their lifestyles and the amount of pictures about alcohol intake these participants had on their Facebook profiles that made them consider this topic as intimate—I would argue that in the sense of private more than intimate. Also information leaks may occur through friends' posts. Thus, these participants may be concerned about the potential damage that pictures portraying them drunk may have upon their reputation.

3.6   FEELINGS AND e-MOTIONS

References to feelings and emotions were common when defining online intimacy and these kinds of disclosures were usually related to the Facebook wall. Feelings on social media may be related to many different topics or relationships. Participants usually referred to the disclosure of feelings in relation to their romantic relationships, their family, or their friends. As discussed in the previous chapter, Viel (38, Spain) explained that he used to write a blog as a kind of diary to jot down his feelings in an anonymous way, since he felt protected by anonymity. Participants usually claimed that they did not understand why people actually posted those kinds of feelings publicly on Facebook. Some of them characterized this practice as inappropriate, because they believed that intimacy should be disclosed privately, as we discussed in the previous chapter. For instance, Vanessa (29, Spain) mentioned that although her partner (Viel) talked about their relationship on Facebook, and sometimes disclosed his feelings towards her online, she would not talk about their feelings on social media. She stated that she would not engage in this kind of disclosure in public because she located those feelings in her private zone.

On the other hand, Qiu et al. (2012) found in their research that Facebook users mainly disclosed positive information in order to display themselves in a better light. Nevertheless, in my study, participants seemed to convey that if they did not post negative feelings, it was because they considered it a claim of attention, as an act of exhibitionism, and they viewed it as socially awkward. For instance:

> One bad thing that one friend of mine published, she had a problem with her ex-boyfriend and she was publicly talking about that. So I think that those kinds of things shouldn't be there. I don't need to know about that. I knew about it because my friend had told me, but I called her and I asked her: why are you putting that on Facebook? (Raquel, 35, Spain)

This is in line with the rule, Köhl and Götzenbrucker (2014, p. 519) argue, that "positive feelings can be shared with others, while negative feelings are to be kept inside". Despite her criticism about publishing about relationship problems in public, Raquel (35, Spain) was one of the few participants who actually posted about her feelings on her Facebook wall, often about negative matters. For instance, she posted that her father died, that she needed a friend, or that she was sad or happy. Moreover, she posted about her experience using dating sites; she was a bit disappointed about it and she complained about a lack of spontaneity on her dates. Raquel tagged me on that post and asked me for my (expert) opinion. In this case her posts were clearly a cry for help and support. Most participants did not engage in these kinds of practices, and some of them questioned why people published their negative feelings online. For example, Gemma, who actually posted "I love you mum" through Facebook, expressed it nicely in the following quote:

> I used to post more things in the past. But sometimes you wonder: "What's Facebook for?" I used to explain more how I was feeling and stuff, but I quit doing it because what are they going to comment: an opinion? Because who really knows how I'm feeling they already know that, I don't need to post it. "What's the objective of posting it: to claim attention, or validation? What for?" So I don't do it. If I feel bad my real friends already know about that, you usually post positive things. (Gemma, 43, Spain)

Apart from Viel, who explained how he openly posted about his love for his partner, most male participants did not disclose their feelings online in writing. In general, participants found the disclosure of feelings and emotions openly through social media as socially inappropriate, especially when those feelings were negative. Contrary to what other studies showed, participants claimed that they did not want to write about their bad emotions online because they found it exhibitionistic and as a cry for help.

Feelings and emotions can be conveyed through textual or visual communication. Lambert (2013), drawing on Berger (1982), suggested that photographs could be considered visual representations of emotions. On Facebook, the public display of feelings and affection towards other people was often expressed through pictures or commenting on them. In particular, most participants found it inappropriate to upload pictures with children. In fact, in Badoo, it is not allowed to upload photos "without you in them, children, erotic or inappropriate." It is common practice to upload intimate pictures with friends or partners and tag them, so the pictures also appear in their profiles (Miguel 2016). This co-construction of the online self is also carried out through comments on those pictures by other users and through references, and they play an important role in how users are perceived by their contacts on the platform.

3.7   CONCLUSIONS

Badoo and CouchSurfing are social media platforms designed to connect people and foster the encounter face to face. Most participants chose to disclose their real identity, as the objective of using those platforms is to meet face to face. Therefore, the potential future meeting made users behave in a relatively honest way. In the search for intimacy, there is always a certain level of exposure that implies vulnerability. Thus, users negotiate the breadth and depth of their disclosures in order to both achieve intimacy and protect themselves from potential harm. The topics most participants considered intimate were relationship status, sexual orientation, political and religious beliefs, alcohol intake, sex, and feelings, which are mainly related to embodiment.

Sexual orientation and relationship status are the kinds of information necessary and expected to be disclosed because the objective of using the platform is to find a partner. Most Badoo participants did not identify those concepts as intimate; I argue that, that may be due to a process of "disclosure domestication". Nevertheless, on Facebook, most participants decided not to disclose these kinds of information because they did not consider them necessary in that context and to prevent existing relationships knowing about their love life. Especially LGBT participants qualified sexual orientation and relationship status as intimate, and expressed their concern about other people knowing about their sexuality through Facebook, although they thought it was adequate to disclose it on a dating platform. In the case of CouchSurfing, in general, sexual orientation was not considered as relevant information to be revealed on the CouchSurfing profile. Only CouchSurfing participants who were living with their partners considered it important to specify their relationship status, as both members of the couple would host potential guests.

In relation to religious and political beliefs there were few participants who disclosed these kinds of information and also a few participants actually identified those topics as intimate. Some of these participants did not disclose their beliefs at all; others felt comfortable publishing their religion or political beliefs online on Facebook, although one participant also expressed his political beliefs through CouchSurfing; and others did not have a clear idea whether their religious and political beliefs were intimate or not. Although male participants linked online intimacy with sex more often than female participants, in general, across all platforms, both male and female participants usually restricted conversations about sex to the chat function and rarely uploaded sexy pictures. Some participants also considered alcohol intake as intimate, in particular participants who often had clear disclosures about their drinking habits on Facebook and CouchSurfing. I argue that these participants identified alcohol intake as intimate due to their lifestyle. Most male participants did not disclose their feelings online in writing. The public display of feelings and affection towards other people were often expressed by uploading pictures. In general, participants found the disclosure of feelings and emotions openly through social media as socially inappropriate, especially when those feelings were negative or were related to relationship problems. Contrary to what other studies found, participants claimed that they did not want to write about their bad emotions online because they found it exhibitionistic.

Apart from the opinions and accounts of some participants about sexy pictures, where female users were expected to self-police their pictures to avoid looking like "sluts", where a clear gender bias can be observed, in general, I did not find significant differences in intimate disclosures in relation to gender or age among participants. What was more relevant in order to define the decision to reveal certain intimate information or not was the type of platform. Sexual orientation and relationship status were conveyed through all platforms, but especially on Badoo, due to its dating nature. Political and religious beliefs and emotions were mainly conveyed through Facebook. Alcohol intake and sex were usually disclosed through Badoo and Facebook. In general, I will conclude that in relation to online communication, CouchSurfing would be the platform where less intimate disclosures can be found. Thus, a participant's decision to disclose different intimate topics in different social media platforms was mainly led by what was needed or sociably desirable on each platform rather than by their consideration of these topics as being intimate or not.

References

Altman, I., & Taylor, D. A. (1973). *Social penetration: The development of interpersonal relationships.* Oxford: Holt, Rinehart & Winston.

Archer, R. L., & Burleson, J. A. (1980). The effects of timing of self-disclosure on attraction and reciprocity. *Journal of Personality and Social Psychology, 38*(1), 120–130.

Bargh, J. A., & McKenna, K. Y. (2004). The Internet and social life. *Annual Review of Psychology, 55*(February), 573–590.

Baym, N. K. (2010). *Personal connection in the digital age.* Cambridge: Polity Press.

Berger, J. (1982). Appearances. In J. Berger & J. Mohr (Eds.), *Another way of telling* (pp. 81–129). New York: Vintage Books.

Brake, D. R. (2014). *Sharing our lives online: Risks and exposure in social media.* London: Palgrave Macmillan.

Cohen, J. E. (2012). *Configuring the networked self: Law, code, and the play of everyday practice.* New Have: Yale University Press.

Ellison, N. B., Vitak, J., Steinfield, C., Gray, R., & Lampe, C. (2011). Negotiation privacy concerns and social capital needs in a social media environment. In S. Trepte & L. Reinecke (Eds.), *Privacy online: Perspective on privacy and self-disclosure on the social web* (pp. 19–32). New York: Springer.

Goffman, E. (1969). *The presentation of self in everyday life.* London: Allen Lane.

Hjorth, L., Wilken, R., & Gu, K. (2012). Ambient intimacy: A case study of the iPhone, presence, and location based social media in Shanghai, China. In L. Hjorth, J. Burgess, & I. Richardson (Eds.), *Studying mobile media: Cultural technologies, mobile communication, and the iPhone* (pp. 43–62). New York: Routledge.

Hogan, B. (2010). The presentation of self in the age of social media: Distinguishing performances and exhibitions online. *Bulletin of Science Technology Society, 30*(6), 377–386.

Illouz, E. (2007). *Cold intimacies: The making of emotional capitalism.* Cambridge: Polity Press.

Jiang, C. L., & Hancock, J. T. (2013). Absence makes the communication grow fonder: Geographic separation, interpersonal media, and intimacy in dating relationships. *The Journal of Communication, 63*(3), 556–577.

Joinson, A. N., Houghton, D. J., Vasalou, A., & Marder, B. L. (2011). Digital crowding: Privacy, self-disclosure, and technology. In S. Trepte & L. Reinecke (Eds.), *Privacy online: Perspectives on privacy and self-disclosure in the social web* (pp. 33–45). Heidelberg: Springer.

Jordán-Conde, Z., Mennecke, B., & Townsend, A. (2013). Late adolescent identity definition and intimate disclosure on Facebook. *Computers in Human Behavior, 33*, 356–366.

Köhl, M. M., & Götzenbrucker, G. (2014). Networked technologies as emotional resources? Exploring emerging emotional cultures on social network sites such as Facebook and Hi5: A trans-cultural study. *Media, Culture & Society, 36*(4), 508–525.

Lambert, A. (2013). *Intimacy and friendship on Facebook.* Basingstoke: Palgrave Macmillan.

Lara, T. (2007). El currículum posmoderno en la cultura. Zemos98.org. [Online]. Available from: http://equipo.zemos98.org/El-curriculum-posmoderno-en-la. Accessed 14 May 2014.

Lasén, A. (2013). Digital inscriptions and loss of embarrassment: Some thoughts about the technological mediations of affectivity. *Intervalla, 1*, 85–100.

Lomborg, S. (2013). *Social media, social genres: Making sense of the ordinary.* New York: Routledge.

Marwick, A. E., & boyd, d. (2011). I tweet honestly, I tweet passionately. Twitter users, context collapse, and the imagined audience. *New Media & Society, 13*(1), 114–133.

Mendelson, A., & Papacharissi, Z. (2010). Look at us: Collective narcissism in college student Facebook photo galleries. In Z. Papacharissi (Ed.), *A networked self: Identity, community, and culture on social network sites* (pp. 251–273). New York: Routledge.

Miguel, C. (2016). Visual intimacy on social media: From selfies to the co-construction of intimacies through shared pictures. *Social Media + Society, 2*(2). https://doi.org/10.1177/2056305116641705.

Miller, D. (2011). *Tales from Facebook.* Cambridge, MA: Polity Press.

Nguyen, M., Bin, Y. S., & Campbell, A. (2012). Comparing online and offline self-disclosure: A systematic review. *Cyberpsychology, Behavior and Social Networking, 15*(2), 103–111.

Nissenbaum, H. (2009). *Privacy in context: Technology, policy, and the integrity of social life.* Stanford: University Press.

Park, N., Jin, B., & Jin, S. A. (2011). Effects of self-disclosure on relational intimacy in Facebook. *Computers in Human Behavior, 27*(5), 1974–1983.

Pedroni, M., Pasquali, F., & Carlo, S. (2014). My friends are my audience: Mass-mediation of personal content and relations in Facebook. *Observatorio (OBS*), 8*(3), 97–113.

Qiu, L., Lin, H., Leung, A. K., & Tov, W. (2012). Putting their best foot forward: Emotional disclosure on Facebook. *Cyberpsychology, Behavior and Social Networking, 15*(10), 569–572.

Reichelt, L. (2007, March 1). 'Ambient intimacy'. Disambiguity. http://www.disambiguity.com/ambient-intimacy/. Accessed 10 Dec 2016.

Reis, H. T., & Shaver, P. (1988). Intimacy as an interpersonal process. In S. Duck (Ed.), *Handbook of personal relationships: Theory, research, and interventions* (pp. 367–389). Oxford: John Wiley & Sons.

Sprecher, S., Treger, S., Wondra, J. D., Hilaire, N., & Wallpe, K. (2013). Taking turns: Reciprocal self-disclosure promotes liking in initial interactions. *Journal of Experimental Social Psychology, 49*(5), 860–866.

Thompson, C. (2008, September 15). Brave new world of digital intimacy. *New York Times Magazine.* [Online]. Available from: http://www.nytimes.com/2008/09/07/magazine/07awareness-t.html. Accessed 5 June 2012.

Thumim, N. (2012). *Self representation and digital culture*. Basingstoke: Palgrave Macmillan.

Utz, S. (2015). The function of self-disclosure on social network sites: Not only intimate, but also positive and entertaining self-disclosures increase the feeling of connection. *Computers in Human Behavior, 45*(April), 1–10.

Walther, J. B. (1996). Computer-mediated communication impersonal, interpersonal, and hyperpersonal interaction. *Communication Research, 23*(1), 3–43.

Walther, J. B., & Parks, M. R. (2002). Cues filtered out, cues filtered in: Computer-mediated communications and relationship. In M. Knapp & J. Daly (Eds.), *Handbook of interpersonal communication* (pp. 529–563). Thousand Oaks: Sage.

Walther, J. B., Van Der Heide, B., Kim, S., Westerman, D., & Tong, S. T. (2008). The role of friends' behavior on evaluations of individuals' Facebook profiles: Are we known by the company we keep? *Human Communication Research, 34*(1), 28–49.

CHAPTER 4

Social Media Platforms as Intimacy Mediators

Abstract The objective of this chapter is to understand the interplay between society and social media. Understanding the way people appropriate technology in their everyday lives is an important step towards better understanding our social world. This chapter presents an analysis of the increasingly invisible process of mediation due to the domestication of new media. The concepts of domestication of technology and mediation are explored in order to explain the process of the pervasive use of social media in everyday life. In addition, the role that platforms' politics and architecture play in shaping the way people communicate and build relationships is analysed. Finally, to provide some contemporary examples, the attention is focused on dating sites and hospitality exchange platforms, using Badoo and CouchSurfing as case studies.

Keywords Badoo • CouchSurfing • Intimacy • Mediation • Online dating • Social media

4.1 Introduction

The new culture of connectivity (Van Dijck 2013) is embedded in our everyday lives and is transforming the way we relate to each other. As Rosenfeld and Thomas (2010, p. 36) put it: "[T]he Internet is a new kind of social intermediary that may reshape the kinds of partners and relationships we have." The increasing mobility of people in the context of a

© The Author(s) 2018   59
C. Miguel, *Personal Relationships and Intimacy in the Age of Social Media*, https://doi.org/10.1007/978-3-030-02062-0_4

globalized world facilitates meeting and interacting with strangers more than ever before. Bialski (2012) points out that these meetings with strangers can also be coordinated through different kinds of social networking sites (SNSs), such as hospitality exchange networks, dating sites, and so on. After the discussion of the concepts of mediation and domestication of technology, I address the politics of platforms. Following Latour's (2005) distinction between mediators and intermediaries, I assert that platforms shape the way people communicate. Finally, I report a brief outline of the short history of Badoo and CouchSurfing, and describe the characteristics of both the sites to understand how they facilitate the creation of personal relationships.

4.2   Social Media Life

The origins of SNSs, as boyd and Ellison (2007) explain, can be traced back to 1995 (Classmates) and 1997 (SixDegrees). SixDegrees included users' profiles, but most major dating sites already allowed users to create profiles. SixDegrees allowed users to list their Friends and, from 1998, surf the Friends lists (ibid.). Each of these features existed in some form before SixDegrees, of course. Nevertheless, the first successful SNSs were Friends Reunited and Friendster, which appeared in 2000 and 2002, respectively, because they allowed users to share pictures with each other. Facebook appeared in 2004 as a university students–only network. It opened to the general public in September 2006 (Facebook 2018). Although other social media platforms such as Twitter, Instagram, and Snapchat have appeared in recent years and reached high popularity, Facebook still remains the SNS with the largest number of users (Alexa 2018a). In fact, SNSs have become some of the most popular sites among users, with Facebook, YouTube, Reddit, Twitter, and Instagram on the top 15 list of the most visited sites in the world (Alexa 2018a).

Through SNSs, users interact with other users and content in different ways. boyd and Ellison (2007, p. 211) provided one of the most popular definitions of SNSs: Social network sites are Web-based services that allow individuals to (1) construct a public or semi-public profile within a bounded system, (2) articulate a list of other users with whom they share a connection, and (3) view and traverse their list of connections and those made by others within the system. Hinton and Hjorth (2013) note that most SNSs include similar features such as profiles (which include (nick) name, picture(s), and biographical information), lists of connections, comments, and private messaging. Hinton and Hjorth (2013, p. 34) explain that some SNSs are "based around a theme", such as LinkedIn (work) or CouchSurfing (travel), while others do not have a particular theme, but they just offer a way to connect to people, such as Google+ or Facebook.

The latest buzzword is social media, which replaces the previous concept of social software. What is social about social media? Fuchs (2014, p. 45) explains that social media are "Web platforms that enable the social networking of people, bring people together and mediate feelings of virtual togetherness". Some authors (e.g., Baym 2010; Standage 2013) have claimed that social media is not a new phenomenon, and has been around for centuries. Standage (2013) points to cavern paintings, poetry, or the telegraph as examples of traditional social media. Social media platforms are interfaces that facilitate connectivity and promote interpersonal contact between strangers, existing relationships, individuals, and groups. These platforms allow users to communicate in public and private ways through different tools such as reference systems, walls, groups, forums, mailboxes, or chats. Van Dijck (2013) suggests that the word "connectivity" implies a technological meaning insomuch as social media platforms allow us to make connections with people through different features such as "chat" or "comments" on pictures. Van Dijck (2013) argues that connectivity has become a human need, as our lives are embedded in technology-mediated communication. The pervasive use of smartphones, which allow us to be connected 24/7 through social media apps, has helped to create this need. In a similar vein, Langlois (2013) highlights the power that social media platforms have achieved in recent years and explains that giving up social media is much more complicated than quitting television, because not only do we use social media for entertainment and information, we also experience our friendship, love, and social life through these platforms.

The culture of "always on" (e.g., Baron 2008, p. 10; Turkle 2008, p. 132) generates new dependencies on devices and services. Following Silverstone and Haddon (1996), who defined domestication as the process through which new technology is integrated into everyday life, Baron (2008) points to smartphones as the main drivers of the domestication of communication technologies. Turkle (2008) observes that these devices are fostering the culture of always-on/always-on-me, where the individual feels connected anytime, anywhere. This *hyperconnected* individual has been labelled as the "tethered self" (Turkle 2008, p. 122) or the "networked self" (Papacharissi 2010, p. 307). Turkle (2007, p. 9) points out that the closeness to our mobile phones creates the feeling that these devices are "intimate machines". Likewise, Miller (2014) suggests that users may feel more emotionally attached to mobile phones because of their close physicality to the device and its affordances. Miller (ibid.) draws on Vincent (2005), who, emulating Marshall McLuhan, argued that for some people, mobile devices may feel like extension of their bodies. Hjorth (2014) has developed a theory of the "caravan" to highlight how these small devices allow us to bring with us our social life everywhere we go; hence, they facilitate co-presence. Hjorth (ibid.) argues that co-presence is a psychological state not limited by physical boundaries. This new media ecology is formed by different devices (desktop computers, mobile phones, and tablets), across different social and media platforms, and creates various forms of presence (Hinton and Hjorth 2013). The convergence of mobile devices with social networking sites opens new opportunities and challenges for interpersonal communication. Race (2015, p. 505), in his research about the role of hook-up apps in gay culture, claims that platforms such as Grindr represent "an historically distinctive way of arranging erotic and intimate life and accessing partners, which has significant social, personal and communal impacts and potentials".

Hine (2015) developed a model to help study the integration of digital communication in our everyday practices: the "E³ Internet framework". This framework defines three aspects of the Internet: embedded, embodied, and everyday. Hine (ibid.) argues that the Internet has become embedded into our lives, interwoven in everyday experiences. First, Hine (ibid.) explains that there are many different notions of embedding within new media in different contexts, for instance, the appropriation by one particular culture of a social media platform. Deuze (2012) stresses how our lives are embedded in media by saying that we live *in* media rather than *with* media. Miller (2014) also acknowledges the extensive penetration of mediated communication in our lives and suggests that people interpret media representations as being part of their reality.

Hine's (2015) second point is that the Internet is embodied, and she highlights the importance of the material circumstances that are shaping the mediated emotional experience. In social media context, Lasén and García (2015, p. 4) explain how self-portraits accomplish three functions: presentation, representation, and embodiment, insofar as they "inscribe the body online and offline". Cohen (2012) observes that the body has usually been neglected in Internet studies and points out that technology does not obliterate embodiment but modifies aspects of embodied experiences, as it is not possible to separate our bodily experience when we use communication technologies.

The third aspect of the use of the Internet identified by Hine (2015) is "everyday". One of the first scholars to study the Internet in the context of everyday interaction was Bakardjieva (2005), who authored *Internet Society: The Internet in Everyday Life*. Bakardjieva (ibid.) highlighted how users contributed to the shaping of technology with their own choices insofar as they integrated the Internet in their everyday practices. The diffusion of broadband capacity and extensive use of mobile communication have resulted in social media interaction penetrating all layers of one's social life (see Castells 2007; Livingstone 2009; Papacharissi 2010; Turkle 2011; Couldry 2012; Deuze 2012; Madianou and Miller 2013). De Ridder (2013) acknowledges that because participation in social media has become an everyday practice, the power structures (both cultural and commercial) embedded in these platforms have become invisible. In his study about mediated intimacy, De Ridder (ibid.) noted that it is important to observe how the pervasive use of new technologies affects intimacy. For example, some authors (e.g., Turkle 2008; Miller 2011) argue that users may feel more attached to social media platforms than to specific friends, as the platform is always available to them, and thus becomes a "metafriend". As Turkle (2008, p. 124) puts it: "The site becomes a transference object, the place where friendship comes from." Nevertheless, instead of thinking about major disruptive transformations in social practices, it is more useful to talk about the integration of new media in everyday routines. As Papacharissi (2010) observes, although several scholars have questioned whether new technologies made users more or less social, the reality is that after an initial first stage of intensive use of new media, users integrate digital technologies in their everyday practices as part of their regular social interaction.

In communication studies, concepts such as mediation and mediatization (e.g., Silverstone 2005; Couldry 2008; Livingstone 2009; Thumim 2012; Madianou and Miller 2013; Lievrouw 2014) have been used to understand the role that media play in contemporary society. Couldry (2008) highlights that the concept of mediation is more adequate to approach the study of media's social consequences at macro and micro levels, in spite of mediatization, which accounts for the political and power forces shaping a process of media influence on a large scale. Livingstone (2009) studied the etymology of both concepts in different languages and concluded that the concept of mediation is useful because it highlights the artefacts and practices present in communication, and stresses the social context where the communication takes place. In her research about self-representation, Thumim (2012) identifies three dimensions that operate in the process of mediation: institutional (e.g., social media companies), textual (through both text and images), and cultural (personal experience).

Communication is always mediated by language, as Silverstone (2005) has observed. Following Silverstone (2005), who described mediation as a dialectical process, in which the media are involved in the general circulation of symbols in social life, Madianou and Miller (2013) point out that the concept of mediation helps us understand how media affect social processes, which, at the same time, shape the way media are used. As Madianou and Miller (2013, p. 174) put it: "[M]ediation tries to capture the ways in which communications media transform social processes while being socially shaped themselves." Couldry (2008) understands the process of mediation as the resultant of the interaction of flows of production, circulation, interpretation, and recirculation. The shift with social media in the context of interpersonal communication is that it makes possible both one-to-one communication and one-to-many communication—what Castells (2007) has labelled mass-self communication. Castells (ibid.) highlights that technology is not the agent that produces this new form of socialization, but the force of an individualistic society that demands this kind of communication.

The mediation framework is useful to understand how the materiality of digital communications (devices and objects, e.g., social media platforms) and communication practices are mutually shaped, Lievrouw (2014) suggests. She also acknowledges that social arrangements, such as patterns of relations and institutional structure, are affected and influenced by artefacts and practices through a process of reformation. Thus, the mediation framework would be composed of three elements: (1) artefacts, (2) practices, and (3) social arrangements, which interact and shape one another.

Taking a social shaping of technology approach (e.g., Wajcman 2002; Baym 2010; Madianou and Miller 2013; Van Dijck 2013), and a domestication perspective (e.g., Bakardjieva 2005; Hine 2015), this research follows the academic interest of the study of the use of social media technology in the context of everyday practices. As Baym (2010) notes, the social shaping of technology perspective concurs with the domestication of technology approach insofar as they state that both technology and society are influencers in the consequences of new media. Nevertheless, the domestication of technology perspective focuses on how this interplay between society and technology is deeply embedded in everyday practices. From the domestication perspective, I take into account the mediation process in order to explore how we live our lives *through* social media, and in particular, how we experience intimacy *through* these platforms. In the next section, I analyse how social media platforms' architecture, design, and politics shape the way people communicate.

4.3   PLATFORM POLITICS, ARCHITECTURE, AND POLICIES

The term "platform" has emerged in recent years as a useful metaphor to define social media services. In the context of digital communication, it was first introduced by O'Reilly (2005, p. 17), who proclaimed that "Web 2.0 is the network as platform" in order to highlight the open and participatory structure of these new services that allowed people to create content and interact in a more horizontal way. The term is helpful in acknowledging social media services' dual social and commercial nature. As Gillespie (2010) puts it, the term "platform" helps one navigate the tensions inherent in their service. Thus, Gillespie (ibid.) points out that social media services adopted the metaphor of platform because it allowed both social and commercial interaction, and could address both advertisers and users at the same time. I consider that social media platforms are not neutral intermediaries of interpersonal communication. In this section, I approach the politics of platforms because their design is carefully crafted to both facilitate personal interaction and gather users' data.

From the point of view that technology is not neutral, several scholars (e.g., Papacharissi 2009; Davis 2010; Gillespie 2010; Bucher 2013; Langlois 2013; Patelis 2013; Van Dijck 2013; Lievrouw 2014) discuss issues of power in reference to social media platform architecture and design. These authors argue that social media platforms are not neutral intermediaries, which just facilitate interpersonal communication, but rather they shape the way people communicate. Van Dijck (2013) highlights the power implication of platforms' design when she affirms that platforms are mediators *rather* than intermediaries. Likewise, Mancinelli and Mancinelli (2013, p. 161) emphasize the role of social media platforms as mediators of users' interaction when they claim that "[t]he machine is a mediator".

In contrast, Gillespie (2010) thinks of platforms as digital intermediaries, although he also acknowledges their politics of shaping users' agency. Likewise, Tierney (2013, p. 77), building on the architect William Mitchell (2000), who analysed how the design of a particular architecture had a particular end in mind, points out that "all the design is political". Van Dijck (2013) argues that social media platforms make sociability technical, although social media companies stress the social aspect over the technical one. Papacharissi (2009) also observes how social media architecture and their networked structure shape the way users interact. Papacharissi (2009), who also draws on Hutchby's (2001) theory of *affordances*, conducted a comparative analysis of Facebook, LinkedIn, and the exclusive, members-only ASmallWorld to examine how architectural features influence community building and identity. She identifies the architecture of Facebook as flexible in comparison to the architecture of LinkedIn and ASmallWorld. Papacharissi (ibid.) argues that LinkedIn and ASmallWorld lead human behaviour in a more specific way, as their architecture is more closed, so they offer fewer options for interaction.

Social media platforms' architecture affects self-presentation and social interaction. Some scholars (e.g., Illouz 2007; Papacharissi 2009; Davis 2010; Bucher 2013; De Ridder 2013; Langlois 2013; Patelis 2013; Van Dijck 2013) claim that platforms' architecture and policies are significant in shaping the way people represent themselves and communicate in social media. The first way of shaping the way people represent themselves in the network is related to the "real name policy" promoted by social media monopolies (e.g., Hogan 2010; Patelis 2013). The pervasive use of "real name policy" by social media platforms has been analysed by different scholars in the context of the philosophy of radical transparency (e.g., McNicol 2013; Patelis 2013; Van Dijck 2013). Since the commercial turn of CouchSurfing, which I discuss further in Chap. 5, the platform enforced real name policy, although they allow users of the old CouchSurfing site to keep using a nickname. Van Dijck (2013) suggests, the norms of radical transparency seem to apply only to users, not to social media companies. According to McNicol (2013), although the disclosure of an authentic self may be beneficial for the development of personal relationships, social media platforms enforce users to use their real name, and describe their interests so their data can be used for targeted advertising. In the contemporary social media landscape, as observed by Patelis (2013) in his study of social media "Terms and Conditions", online identities are considered an extension of real social life. Identity play and anonymity, which were the normal means of online interaction in the 1990s, argues Patelis (ibid.), have become stigmatized, as they are understood as "fake". By the same token, Papacharissi (2009) questions how this shift from the use of pseudonyms to real names in online settings constrains the previously understood liberating aspect of online interaction.

The next step, after choosing which name to disclose, is to fill the fixed categories that social media platforms facilitate to represent the user in the network. De Ridder (2013), in his study about intimacy practices through the Belgian social media platform Netlog, where profiles provide only closed categories to describe personal characteristics, found that users felt constrained by platform architecture when representing themselves. Bucher (2013), in her study of engineered sociality through Facebook, argues that social media platforms need these fixed set of standards because of their underlining algorithmic logic. Davis (2010), who analysed the design of MySpace, suggests that in this platform the open-ended "About Me" section helps users to represent their identity in a freer way. On the other hand, other studies, such as Illouz's (2007) profile analysis of dating sites with open "About Me" sections, reveal that users tend to recreate cultural standards and tend to disclose what they think is expected from them, thus creating very similar and standardized self-presentations. Thus, although an open-ended "About Me" section may give the impression of liberty to describe one's self, the reality is that users are mainly constrained by the social norms that operate in the site, which are even more powerful than the platform's features, as Van Dijck (2013) also discusses.

In social media platforms the default is social, as boyd (2008) notes, insofar as it is easier to share than to hide information. Following Feenberg (2008), who referred to the defaults of design as "constitutive bias", Brake (2014) highlights how the defaults affect users' behaviours. Tierney (2013) observes that most social media platforms are designed to promote users to expose plenty of information about their lives. Social media architecture invites us to disclose a lot of information to participate in the service, and also encourages us, Senft (2012) argues, to monitor the activities of others. Other authors have labelled this activity of watching one another as "lateral surveillance" (Andrejevic 2005, p. 481), or "social surveillance" (Marwick 2012, p. 378). In order to try to control the access of different publics to personal information disclosed in the profile, most popular social media platforms incorporate privacy settings. From basic public/private options to more advanced features in the case of Facebook, such as the friends list (which can be applied to status updates and photos) or private groups, privacy settings are designed to permit users to control with whom they share information (e.g., Baron 2008; Trepte 2015). As Trepte (2015) observes, the configuration of privacy settings allows the negotiation of personal relationships.

On the other hand, social media services shape the way users relate to each other through particular features. Bucher (2013, p. 487) explains, with features such as "two friends' shared history", Facebook tries to bring to present past memories in order to "induce and simulate the emotional and intimate connections seen as a defining feature of friendship". Another feature designed by Facebook to assist personal relationships is the "like button". Bucher (2013, p. 485) suggests that as the maintenance of close relationships is time-consuming, the like button helps users to validate their friendships: "With the like button Facebook made paying attention to friends a one-click sentiment." Conversely, as Gürses and Díaz (2013) observe, social media services also hide certain activities to avoid negative feelings, for example, when users unfriend each other.

In terms of and how algorithms influence the way people communicate through social media, Bucher (2013) introduces the concept of *algorithmic friendship* in order to examine the ways social media platforms engineer techno-sociality. Social media platforms use algorithms to recommend content of particular users who are supposed to be more interesting to them. For example, as Van Dijck (2013, p. 49) has observed, Facebook uses the algorithms EdgeRank and GraphRank in order to filter data produced by the users and "shape them into a meaningful stream of information for that specific user". What Van Dijck finds problematic is that users do not know how the filter works. In this sense, users lack the freedom to customize their newsfeeds as they please. It is the platform that is leading the communication process, favouring the content of some "friends" over others. Langlois (2013, p. 54) also considers that the objective of social media platforms is to shape the way we interrelate to each other: "Their purpose is to tell us what we should do, what we want, how we should feel, who should be our next friend, and so on."

The real interest of social media companies, Langlois (2013) argues, is to generate meaningful experiences by connecting users to other users and relevant information, so users keep using the service and the platform keeps gathering users' data. Thus, Langlois (ibid.) suggests that these meaningful experiences are responsible for our attachment to social media services. Hearn (2010) considers social media platforms as feeling-intermediaries, where the expression of feeling in social media interaction is mined for value. Likewise, Gehl (2013) conducted a study about Facebook's surveillance of users' activity and noted how social media platforms' architecture is designed to gather users' behavioural data. He highlights the affective dimension of social media interaction. According to Gehl (2013), the recording of all these feelings through social media can be considered as an "archive of affect" (2013, p. 228).

Most of the previous discussion about how platform architecture shapes the way people communicate and negotiate personal relationships was based on research conducted about Facebook. To contribute to this debate, I open the discussion to online dating and hospitality exchange platforms. The two social media platforms where I mainly focused my attention were Badoo and CouchSurfing. In order to contextualize the analysis, I provide some background information about these social media platforms in the next sections, followed by an analysis of the platforms' architecture and a discussion of how users negotiate personal relationships through them.

4.4   Dating/Hook-up Sites: The Badoo Case

As stated on its "About" section (Badoo 2018a), Badoo was launched in 2006 by a small international group of young, forward-thinking programmers and is owned by the Russian entrepreneur Andrey Andreev. It is managed from London, Moscow, and Malta, but the company is registered in Cyprus. Badoo is a social media platform where users look for interaction with strangers primarily for hook-ups or dates, although on its website the company claims that "[w]e bring social networking to life by allowing you to chat, make new friends, share photos, maybe even date" (Badoo 2018a). Badoo (ibid.) asserts to be the largest social network for meeting new people locally in the world, with more than 390 million users, located mainly in Italy, France, Spain, Brazil, and Poland (Alexa 2018b). On average, Badoo users spend ten hours a week in the app (Badoo 2018b).

In Badoo, user profiles include a number of pictures; a field to specify whether the user is in the platform to make new friends, chat, or date (the default setting); a description; interests; personal info (including sexual orientation, relationship status, and drinking habits, among other); and languages. Badoo allows users to contact people who live in different locations (through a searcher) or people nearby (if the GPS feature is activated), where users can select the number of miles to search around. Also, users can filter among all, new, or "online now" profiles. The communication happens through the chat feature. User profiles can be added to favourites and users can play to "Encounters", where they can click the heart symbol if they like the user or the "X" if they do not. There is also a crush bottom (a heart with an arrow) to show special interest in another user. It is possible to connect with Facebook to find existing contacts on Badoo. The basic service is free, although there are also premium paid options, which I address extensively in Chap. 5.

When users buy any of the premium services, their accounts appear as verified (since their identity has been checked through their credit card number). Also, users can verify their accounts with their phone number or other social media such as Facebook or Twitter. In this study, only a few participants were verified, mainly through their phone number, Google+, or Facebook. If the name provided on Badoo is different to the one in the social platform used to verify the account, Badoo suggests the user to use the same name in order to not be perceived as fake. Nevertheless, the ease with which one can create other false social media accounts makes this system ineffective as a verification tool. Despite social media platforms increasingly implementing real name policies, there are still some users who prefer to use nicknames. Ana (35, UK) uses her middle name on Badoo, which works as a nickname. In this way, the anonymity facilitated by the use of a nickname led her to communicate intimate details about her life, whilst not disclosing information that could identify her. Although she publishes her own pictures on the site, she explained that the perceived anonymity helped her to open up.

In terms of privacy settings, Badoo offers users to show their profile to any user (public), to members only, or "only to people I like and visit", and decide whether others can share the profile, show distance, show the online status, or allow search by email. The settings are public by default; as commented earlier, the default design fosters specific practices—in this case more visibility would foster more interactions in the platform. Photos can be set as private and the other users who want to see private pictures need to request permission to the user, although in this study participants did not have any private album.

There are few academic studies that analyse interaction through Badoo. Giglietto (2008) conducted a comparative study of Facebook and Badoo in Italy, where Badoo was very popular at the time. Giglietto polled 1600 people by telephone and a random sample of 226 Facebook and Badoo users. Giglietto concluded that Badoo users mainly use the site to make new friends, and that they lack a clear understanding of the invisible audience and underestimate the exposure of their online published content. On the other hand, Martínez-Lirola (2012), who conducted a study focused on linguistic analysis of online communication through the chat function in Spain, states that the two main objectives of Badoo are meeting people who have similar interests or finding a partner. Martínez-Lirola (ibid.) describes Badoo as a hybrid between closed social networks like Facebook and dating sites like Match.com. In her analysis of the online conversation through participant observation, where Martínez-Lirola talked to 150 male Badoo users, she found that on Badoo, men take the initiative in conversations and relationships, reproducing the traditional patterns of starting relationships. I will discuss this topic in Sect. 6.4. The study conducted by Lasén and García (2015) about the use of sexy selfies includes Badoo as one of its case studies. Interestingly, these two last studies are both focused on the male perception of Badoo interaction: the first through text, and the second through selfies.

In this study, most participants explained that they mainly contacted other users to flirt and find some dates. In fact, one participant explained that he tried to contact other men to make some friends, but they did not reply. Like Markham (1998) found in her research about virtual worlds, my participants may have different concepts of online settings: as "mediums", "tools", or "places". Participants also related to Badoo as a substitute of a club, and they reported that it was easier and more comfortable for them to look for dates through Badoo from home than going out to find them. For instance, Ana (35, UK) referred to the possibility of classifying what she wanted as an advantage of using the platform. She also pointed to her age as a factor in her decision to start using dating platforms, because she felt she did not fit into the clubbing scene anymore.

In relation to dating, CouchSurfing seems to be a more successful platform for finding a (sexual) partner than is Badoo, since some participants highlighted that the atmosphere in CouchSurfing meetings is more relaxed for dating because it is not the main objective of participating in the meeting; therefore, people do not feel the pressure to behave in a "dating mode". Most participants who were users of both sites commented that they did not find anyone interesting on Badoo; meanwhile, they found a lot of interesting people on CouchSurfing: "It seems that it's easier to find a partner on CouchSurfing than on Badoo. Badoo is just for sex" (Raquel, 35, Spain).

4.5   HOSPITALITY EXCHANGE/MEET-UP NETWORKS: THE COUCHSURFING CASE

In the 1990s, a number of Web-based hospitality exchange networks appeared, mainly focused on specific groups such as cyclists, women, or hitchhikers. In January 2004, Casey Fenton (along with other co-founders) launched CouchSurfing, a social media platform with a system that enables a user to identify and find someone to provide sleeping space in his or her home for free (O'Regan 2009). CouchSurfing worked as a charity and was run mainly by volunteers until 2011, when it received $7 million from venture capitalists and became a corporation. Many of its users have shown their disapproval of the commercial turn that the platform has taken (Feldman 2012). In last years, the owners have been trying to design a new business model in order to monetize the traffic of the site. CouchSurfing counts more than 14 million users (CouchSurfing 2018). Most users are located in the USA, France, Italy, Germany, and China (Alexa 2018c), and they live mainly in big cosmopolitan cities. CouchSurfing consists of a group of strangers who can see each other's profiles, and make requests to stay at someone else's house or join groups to ask for information, meet up, and share hobbies and interests. There is a main group in most big cities. A weekly meeting and other kind of events and nights out are organized through this group. There are also many different groups in every city organized around different topics (cinema, sports, wine tasting, language exchange, etc.) designed for members to be able to meet up with like-minded people (Miguel and Medina 2011) as well as the feature "hang outs" to find meet-ups in specific locations.

Apart from a profile picture, the name of the user, the location, and the status (Accepting guests, Maybe accepting guests, Wants to meet up, or Not accepting guests), CouchSurfing profiles include a number of sections: About, My Home (description of the number of people the user is willing to host, description of the house, sleeping arrangements, etc.), Photos, References, Friends, and Favourites. Users can use the searcher on the top of the site to find hosts, members, travellers, events, groups, or advice in specific locations. Homophily was identified as an operating factor in the CouchSurfing interaction when selecting whom users want to host or surf with. As Bialski (2013) found in her ethnographic study of trust, users of these services usually choose to interact with people who are similar to them. Although looking for cultural differences, users often prefer to host people of the same age range who have similar interests, and similarly, it is common practice to apply the age filter in the browser when searching for hosts. According to Bialski (ibid.), references play a very important role in deciding whom to interact with. Teng et al. (2010) examined online reputation systems, using CouchSurfing as one case study. They assert that the way of rating other users should not be so public because when users do not have a good experience with another *couchsurfer*,[1] they usually do not leave a bad reference in order to avoid receiving a bad reference in return. Thus, the reputation system is not very useful because it only reflects good experiences. I examine the workings of reputation and verification systems more in depth somewhere else (Miguel 2017). References help to build trust, but also, in some occasions, to signify intimacy among members. The way participants negotiate their use of references on CouchSurfing is a good example of how they usually prefer not to talk about their intimate experiences with other couchsurfers in public, as we discussed in Chap. 2. For instance, in the cases where participants who had a fling left references to each other, they did it in a concealed way, so other users would not fully understand what had happened between them, what boyd and Marwick (2011, p. 22) label 'social steganography'.

Another security feature that CouchSurfing provides is the verification system. In order to verify their identity and location, users pay $25 so that their credit card information can be verified. When CouchSurfing receives the payment and checks the user's identity, a green check symbol appears in the user's profile with the text "payment verified". Then, users receive a code by postal mail to verify their address. Once the users enter this code in their profile, a green symbol appears under the profile picture. Despite some female users expressing security concerns during the hospitality exchange (topic that I cover further in Chap. 6), most participants did not verify their accounts.

On CouchSurfing, Bialski (2012) argues, not only do users reveal personal information such as telephone numbers and addresses with their potential guests, they also share their private space with them. Rosen et al. (2011), in their study about community building on CouchSurfing, found that its users struggle against many common social norms by welcoming strangers into their homes. Bialski has conducted extensive research about intimacy and trust among strangers through CouchSurfing in the context of mobility and hospitality exchange. Bialski (2012, p. 252) concludes that through CouchSurfing users may find moments of closeness and inti-

---

[1] CouchSurfing user.

macy, but, at the same time, there are uncomfortable situations that the users may face: "Awkwardness is another common product of these meetings, often reflecting the power relationship between host and guest."

The original objective of CouchSurfing was hospitality exchange; nevertheless, lately the sociality developed through "groups" and "hangouts" has also become very central to the service. The CouchSurfing platform allows the creation of groups around interests (e.g., Barcelona Wine Lovers, Leeds Language Exchange), so people can join these groups and organize activities together around shared hobbies. CouchSurfing weekly meetings are organized in the main cities. These meetings were a very important part of the social life of some interviewees. In relation to dating, the fact that CouchSurfing users share certain values such as a love for travelling, open-mindedness, and an interest in other cultures, some participants argued, makes the platform more suitable for finding potential partners than the big variety that you might find on a dating platform. Most participants, especially male couchsurfers, observed that they preferred to host (or be hosted by) the opposite sex (or other women, in case of the participant identified as lesbian) because, as some participants noted, "deeply inside people look for a fling" (Gemma, 43, Spain). In addition, female participants highlighted that at the beginning of starting to use the platform, they used to contact only female, or equally male and female users, but that after several experiences receiving none or very low response from female couchsurfers, they just wrote to male users because it was much easier to find a host.

4.6   Conclusions

The technically mediated interaction provided by social media platforms has become so integrated in everyday practices that it has turned invisible through a process of domestication. We use social media platforms to forge intimate and more superficial relationships, which range from friendship, romantic, familial, professional, or hobby-related relationships. So far, I have analysed the role of social media platforms' architecture and their algorithms in shaping the way people communicate within them. Taking the perspective that technology is not neutral, I argue that social media platforms emerge as mediators *rather* than as intermediaries. I have paid special attention to how these platforms allow and engineer personal relationships. The affordances and design of the platform permit users to communicate and share content and, at the same time, shape the way they present themselves in the network, and the way they create and maintain close relationships.

In order to understand how social media platforms shape the way to create new relationships, I have focused on two case studies: Badoo (online dating/hook-up platform) and CouchSurfing (hospitality exchange/meet-up platform). I have analysed the design and features of these platforms and discussed how participants utilize them. Badoo is a chat-based social media platform used to meet new people and interact with them on a one-to-one basis through the chat feature. Badoo is mainly used for hook-up and dating practices. CouchSurfing and Badoo facilitate encounters online and offline, and they are only for adults. On both social media platforms users disclose personal information such as personality, interests, and the kind of people they like, usually accompanied by a number of pictures. Thus, as Lasén and Gómez-Cruz (2009) point out, individuals display their intimacy online through narratives and self-portraits to be scrutinized by different publics, while trying to keep the audience interested in order to increase opportunities for encounters online, offline, or both. As advantages of using online dating platforms, some participants valued the convenience of meeting people without leaving home or spending money on drinks that dating platforms provided. Others mentioned the possibility of applying filters to choose potential friends or partners with similar interests. This focus on agency and freedom to create new relationships through social media runs away from nostalgic perspectives where the erosion of strong ties within the local community is seen as negative and driving to isolation (e.g., Putman 2001). In the case of CouchSurfing, references played a key role to generate trust among users, but also were tools that couchsurfers could use to signify intimacy. In general, participants accepted the platforms as they are because they take their design for granted and learn how to navigate them to achieve their personal goals. In particular, participants in this study valued these social media platforms as intimacy mediators insofar as they provided them with a space to create and maintain personal relationships.

REFERENCES

Alexa. (2018a). *Top sites*. http://www.alexa.com/topsites. Date Accessed 15 June 2018.

Alexa. (2018b). *Traffic of Badoo.com*. http://www.alexa.com/siteinfo/badoo.com. Date Accessed 3 June 2018.

Alexa. (2018c). *Traffic of Couchsurfing.com*. http://www.alexa.com/siteinfo/couchsurfing.com. Date Accessed 15 June 2018.

Andrejevic, M. (2005). The work of watching one another: Lateral surveillance, risk, and governance. *Surveillance & Society, 2*(4), 479–497.

Badoo. (2018a). *About Badoo*. https://badoo.com/en/help/?section=1. Date Accessed 3 June 2018.

Badoo. (2018b). *How Long Are British Millennials Spending on Dating Apps?* https://badoo.com/team/press/105/. Date Accessed 17 June 2018.

Bakardjieva, M. (2005). *Internet society: The Internet in everyday life*. London: Sage Publications.

Baron, N. (2008). *Always on: Language in an online and mobile world*. Oxford: Oxford University Press.

Baym, N. K. (2010). *Personal connection in the digital age*. Cambridge: Polity Press.

Bialski, P. (2012). Online to offline social networking. Contextualising sociality today through couchsurfing.org. In D. Picard & S. Buchberger (Eds.), *Couchsurfing cosmopolitanisms. Can tourism make a better world?* (pp. 161–172). Bielefeld: Transcript Verlag.

Bialski, P. (2013). Not on my couch. The limitations of sharing in the age of collaborative travel and hospitality networks. In *RC21 Conference, 29/31 August 2013, Berlin*. http://www.rc21.org/conferences/berlin2013/RC21-Berlin-Papers/non%20pdf/31-Bialski.doc. Date Accessed 22 Feb 2014.

boyd, d. (2008). Facebook's privacy trainwreck: Exposure, invasion, and social convergence. *Convergence, 14*(1), 13–20.

boyd, d., & Ellison, N. B. (2007). Social network sites: Definition, history, and scholarship. *Journal of Computer-Mediated Communication, 13*(1), 210–230.

boyd, d., & Marwick, A. (2011). Social steganography: Privacy in networked publics. In *61st Annual International Communication Association Conference, 26/30 May 2011, Boston, MA*.

Brake, D. R. (2014). *Sharing our lives online: Risks and exposure in social media*. London: Palgrave Macmillan.

Bucher, T. (2013). The friendship assemblage investigating programmed sociality on Facebook. *Television & New Media, 14*(6), 479–493.

Castells, M. (2007). Communication, power and counter-power in the network society. *International Journal of Communication, 1*(1), 238–266.

Cohen, J. E. (2012). *Configuring the networked self: Law, code, and the play of everyday practice*. New Have: Yale University Press.

CouchSurfing. (2018). *About CouchSurfing*. https://www.couchsurfing.com/about/about-us/. Date Accessed 8 June 2018.

Couldry, N. (2008). Mediatization or mediation? Alternative understandings of the emergent space of digital storytelling. *New Media & Society, 10*(3), 373–391.

Couldry, N. (2012). *Media, society, world: Social theory and digital media practice.* Cambridge: Polity Press.

Davis, J. (2010). Architecture of the personal interactive homepage: Constructing the self through MySpace. *New Media & Society, 12*(7), 1103–1119.

De Ridder, S. (2013). Are digital media institutions shaping youth's intimate stories? Strategies and tactics in the social networking site Netlog. *New Media & Society, 24,* 1–19.

Deuze, M. (2012). *Media life.* Cambridge: Polity Press.

Facebook. (2018). *Company Info.* https://newsroom.fb.com/company-info/. Date Accessed 13 June 2018.

Feenberg, A. (2008). From critical theory of technology to the rational critique of rationality. *Social Epistemology, 22*(1), 5–28.

Feldman, Z. (2012). Beyond freedom and oppression: Social media, refusal and the politics of participation. In *IR 13.0 Conference of the AoIR, 18/21 October 2012, Salford.* http://spir.aoir.org/index.php/spir/article/viewFile/6/pdf. Date Accessed 18 Feb 2015.

Fuchs, C. (2014). *Social media: A critical introduction.* London: Sage Publications.

Gehl, R. W. (2013). "Why I left Facebook": Stubbornly refusing to not exist even after opting out of Mark Zuckerberg's social graph. In G. Lovink & M. Rasch (Eds.), *Unlike us reader: Social media monopolies and their alternatives* (pp. 220–238). Amsterdam: Institute of Network Cultures.

Giglietto, F. (2008). The Italian way to SNSs: A comparison between Badoo and Facebook [PowerPoint presentation]. In: *IR 9.0 Conference: Rethinking Communities, Rethinking Place,* 15/18 October, Copenhagen.

Gillespie, T. (2010). The politics of "platforms". *New Media & Society, 12*(3), 347–364.

Gürses, S., & Díaz, C. (2013). Two tales of privacy in online social networks. *Security & Privacy, 11*(3), 29–37.

Hearn, A. (2010). Structuring feeling: Web 2.0, online ranking and rating, and the digital "reputation" economy. *Ephemera, 10*(3/4), 421–438.

Hine, C. (2015). *Ethnography for the Internet: Embedded, embodied and everyday.* London: Bloomsbury Publishing.

Hinton, S., & Hjorth, L. (2013). *Understanding social media.* London: Sage Publications.

Hjorth, L. (2014). Co-presence and ambient play: A case study of mobile gaming. In M. Berry & M. Schleser (Eds.), *Mobile media making in an age of smartphones* (pp. 48–57). New York: Palgrave Pivot.

Hogan, B. (2010). The presentation of self in the age of social media: Distinguishing performances and exhibitions online. *Bulletin of Science, Technology & Society, 30*(6), 377–386.

Hutchby, I. (2001). *Conversation and technology: From the telephone to the internet.* Oxford: Wiley.

Illouz, E. (2007). *Cold intimacies: The making of emotional capitalism*. Cambridge: Polity Press.

Langlois, G. (2013). Social media, or towards a political economy of psychic like. In G. Lovink & M. Rasch (Eds.), *Unlike us reader: Social media monopolies and their alternatives* (pp. 50–60). Amsterdam: Institute of Network Cultures.

Lasén, A., & García, A. (2015). "...but I haven't got a body to show": Self-pornification and male mixed feelings in digitally mediated seduction practices. *Sexualities, 18*(5–6), 714–730.

Lasén, A., & Gómez-Cruz, E. (2009). Digital photography and picture sharing: Redefining the public/private divide. *Knowledge, Technology & Policy, 2*(3), 205–215.

Latour, B. (2005). *Reassembling the social: An introduction to actor network theory*. Oxford: Oxford University Press.

Lievrouw, L. (2014). Materiality and media in communication and technology studies: An unfinished project. In T. Gillespie, P. J. Boczkowski, & K. A. Foot (Eds.), *Media technologies: Essays on communication, materiality, and society* (pp. 21–52). Cambridge, MA: MIT Press.

Livingstone, S. (2009). On the mediation of everything. *Journal of Communication, 59*(1), 1–18.

Madianou, M., & Miller, D. (2013). Polymedia: Towards a new theory of digital media in interpersonal communication. *International Journal of Cultural Studies, 16*(2), 169–187.

Mancinelli, I., & Macinelli, T. (2013). The Facebook aquarium: Freedom in a profile. In G. Lovink & M. Rasch (Eds.), *Unlike us reader: Social media monopolies and their alternatives* (pp. 159–165). Amsterdam: Institute of Network Cultures.

Markham, A. N. (1998). *Life online: Researching real experience in virtual space*. Walnut Creek: Rowman Altamira.

Martínez-Lirola, M. (2012). Aproximación a la interacción virtual: El caso de la red social Badoo. *Palabra Clave/Keyword, 15*(1), 107–127.

Marwick, A. E. (2012). The public domain: Social surveillance in everyday life. *Surveillance & Society, 9*(4), 378–393.

Miguel, C., & Medina, P. (2011). The transformation of identity and privacy through online social networks (the CouchSurfing case). In *McLuhan Galaxy Conference: Understanding Media Today, 23/25 May 2011, Barcelona* (pp. 331–342). Barcelona: Editorial Universitat Oberta de Catalunya.

Miguel, C. (2017). Beyond engineered intimacy: Navigating social media platforms to manage intimate relationships. In R. Andreassen, M. Nebeling, K. H. Petersen, & T. Raun (Eds.), *Mediated intimacies. Connectivities, relationalities and proximities*. London: Routledge.

Miller, D. (2011). *Tales from Facebook*. Cambridge, MA: Polity Press.

Miller, J. (2014). The fourth screen: Mediatization and the smartphone. *Mobile Media & Communication, 2*(2), 209–226.

Mitchell, W. J. (2000). *E-topia: "Urban life, Jim-but not as we know it"*. Cambridge, MA: MIT Press.

McNicol, A. (2013). None of your business? Analyzing the legitimacy and effects of gendering social spaces through system design. In G. Lovink & M. Rasch (Eds.), *Unlike us reader: Social media monopolies and their alternatives* (pp. 200–219). Amsterdam: Institute of Network Cultures.

O'Regan, M. (2009). Hospitality exchange clubs and the changing nature of tourism and identity. In M. Foucault, L. H. Martin, H. Gutman, & P. H. Hutton (Eds.), *Digital technologies of the self* (pp. 171–198). Newcastle: Cambridge Scholars Publishing.

O'Reilly, T. (2005, September 30). *What is Web 2.0? Design patterns and business models for the next generation of software*. O'Reilly Media, Inc. [Online]. Available from: http://www.oreilly.com/pub/a//web2/archive/what-is-web-20.html. Accessed 13 July 2014.

Papacharissi, Z. (2009). The virtual geographies of social networks: A comparative analysis of Facebook, LinkedIn and ASmallWorld. *New Media & Society, 11*(1–2), 199–220.

Papacharissi, Z. (2010). Conclusion: A networked self. In Z. Papacharissi (Ed.), *A networked self: Identity, community, and culture on social network sites*. London: Routledge.

Patelis, K. (2013). Political economy and monopoly abstractions: What social media demand. In G. Lovink & M. Rasch (Eds.), *Unlike us reader: Social media monopolies and their alternatives* (pp. 117–126). Amsterdam: Institute of Network Cultures.

Putman, R. (2001). *Bowling alone: The collapse and revival of American community*. New York: Simon and Schister.

Race, K. (2015). Speculative pragmatism and intimate arrangements: Online hook-up devices in gay life. *Culture, Health & Sexuality, 17*(4), 496–511.

Rosen, D., Roy Lafontaine, P., & Hendrickson, B. (2011). CouchSurfing: Belonging and trust in a globally cooperative online social network. *New Media & Society, 13*(6), 981–998.

Rosenfeld, M. J., & Thomas, R. J. (2010). *Meeting online: The rise of the Internet as a social intermediary*. Unpublished manuscript, Stanford. [Online]. Available from: http://www.iga.ucdavis.edu/Research/EJS/Rosenfeld%20paper.pdf. Accessed 12 July 2013.

Senft, T. M. (2012). Microcelebrity and the branded self. In J. Burgess & A. Bruns (Eds.), *Blackwell companion to new media dynamics* (pp. 346–654). Oxford: Blackwell.

Silverstone, R., & Haddon, L. (1996). Design and the domestication of ICTs: Technical change and everyday life. In R. Silverstone & R. Mansell (Eds.), *Communication by design: The politics of information and communication technologies* (pp. 44–74). Oxford: Oxford University Press.

Silverstone, R. (2005). The sociology of mediation and communication. In C. Calhoun, C. Rojeck, & B. Turner (Eds.), *The SAGE handbook of sociology* (pp. 188–207). London: Sage Publications.

Standage, T. (2013). *Writing on the wall: Social media-the first two thousand years.* London: Bloomsbury Publishing.

Teng, C., Lauterbach, D., & Adamic, L.A. (2010). "I rate you. You rate me": Should we do so publicly? In: 3rd Workshop on online social networks, 22/25 June, Boston. https://www.usenix.org/legacy/event/wosn10/tech/full_papers/Teng.pdf. Accessed 23 Feb 2012.

Thumim, N. (2012). *Self representation and digital culture.* Basingstoke: Palgrave Macmillan.

Tierney, T. (2013). *The public space of social media: Connected cultures of the network society.* New York: Routledge.

Trepte, S. (2015). Social media, privacy, and self-disclosure: The turbulence caused by social media's affordances. *Social Media + Society, 1*(1), 1–2.

Turkle, S. (2007). *Evocative objects: Things that matter.* Cambridge, MA: MIT Press.

Turkle, S. (2008). Always-on/always-on-you: The tethered self. In J. E. Katz (Ed.), *Handbook of mobile communication studies* (pp. 121–137). Cambridge, MA: MIT Press.

Turkle, S. (2011). *Alone together: Why we expect more from technology and less from each other.* New York: Basic Books.

Van Dijck, J. (2013). *The culture of connectivity: A critical history of social media.* Oxford: Oxford University Press.

Vincent, J. (2005). Emotional attachment to mobile phones an extraordinary relationship. In L. Hamill & A. Lasén (Eds.), *Mobile world: Past, present and future* (pp. 93–104). Bern: Peter Lang.

Wajcman, J. (2002). Addressing technological change: The challenge to social theory. *Current Sociology, 50*(3), 347–363.

CHAPTER 5

The Political Economy of Networked Intimacy

Abstract This chapter analyses Web 2.0 technologies and their pervasive imperative of sharing under the culture of participation. It explores the political economy of social media platforms in relation to intimacy, insofar as they facilitate the creation and development of close relationships but, at the same time, profit from these intimate relationships through data mining or charging a fee to access the service or to use premium services. In order to stress the connections between the political economy of social media companies and the intimacy practices they facilitate, this chapter examines the business models of Badoo, CouchSurfing, and Facebook, including participants' perceptions on the ways these companies monetize their traffic and the market intervention in the creation of new relationships.

Keywords Intimacy • Platforms • Political economy • Sharing • Social media

5.1 Introduction

This chapter explores the evolving concept of sharing in the context of social media interaction and analyses how social media platforms have shaped the way people communicate by promoting self-disclosure. Following Hinton and Hjorth (2013, p. 11), I use the concept of Web 2.0 as a placeholder to discuss the political economy of social media because

© The Author(s) 2018   81
C. Miguel, *Personal Relationships and Intimacy in the Age of Social Media*, https://doi.org/10.1007/978-3-030-02062-0_5

"Web 2.0 is a term that is fundamentally derived from the logic of capitalism, marketing and commercialisation". Here, I discuss how Web 2.0 services are based on the imperative of sharing. I first analyse the characteristics of Web 2.0 technologies. Then, I will explore the mobilization of the concept of sharing, by looking at social media companies' communications and rhetorics, where they draw on the emotional connotations of the concept of sharing. I also discuss the political economy of these platforms in relation to intimacy, insofar as they facilitate the creation and development of close relationships but, at the same time, profit from these intimate relationships through data mining or charging a fee to access the service or to use premium services. Thus, I analyse the role of social media companies in this new scenario of constant connectivity, which involves, as Hinton and Hjorth (2013) observe, a double logic of empowerment and commodification. Finally, I present a discussion about the monetization of intimacy in the context of social media.

5.2   Web 2.0 and the Imperative of Sharing

From 2005 the term Web 2.0 acquired a lot of repercussion. The term was first defined by O'Reilly (2005) in his article "What Is Web 2.0? Design Patterns and Business Models for the Next Generation of Software". As Fuchs (2014) notes, it suddenly became a buzzword in order to talk about SNSs, wikis, video- and photo-sharing platforms, and other sites that allowed the user to participate in the service by creating new content and interacting with other users. Web 2.0 technologies is based on social software (So-So). Fuchs (2014, p. 35) defines social software as "the software that enables individuals and communities to gather, communicate, share and in some cases collaborate or play". Web 2.0 business models blend participatory and commercial philosophy. In the participatory culture, the connotations of equality, selflessness, and giving, which connect with discourses of the philosophy of the utopian network culture from the 1980s and 1990s, are combined with the ideal mode of communication between intimates. Social media companies use the communitarian ideology from the early stages of the Internet in their slogans and communications, borrowing terminology from the Internet free-culture ideology based on values such as altruism, reciprocity, and collaborative knowledge, which I addressed in Chap. 1.

O'Reilly (2005, p. 17), who coined the term Web 2.0, highlights that Web 2.0 is based on the idea of the "web as platform" which is built around "architecture of participation". One of the benefits of Web 2.0 is that it allows people to share and exchange ideas and goods. At the same time, this logic has been appropriated by social media companies to create their business models. Using a critical political economy approach, Van Dijck and Nieborg (2009) criticize these celebratory views of the "participatory culture", arguing that they do not take into account the commodity logic underneath Web 2.0 companies. Other scholars (e.g., Van Dijck and Nieborg 2009; John 2013a; Dror 2013; Kennedy 2013; Brake 2014) have also analysed how social media companies use communitarian and emotional pitches to encourage users to share more information online. Van Dijck and Nieborg (2009) discuss how Web 2.0 open philosophy appropriated the communitarian "network culture" ideology to market these new platforms in a positive and attractive way to their potential users, despite these social media monopolies using user-generated content for profit. Dror (2013) examined high-profile Web 2.0 companies' founders' manifestos and found that these documents faced the challenge of having to address venture capitalists, advertisers, and general public with the same discourse. Dror (2013, p. 11–12) explains how these founders solved this challenge by addressing different stakeholders using an emotional speech by using slogans such as "make the world a better place" or "give everyone a voice".

Social media platforms encourage people to share different kinds of creative content and details of their lives in public as a differentiating mechanism from one another in order to create self-branded identities, which are used to navigate technologically mediated relationships. Brake (2014), in his empirical work about risk and exposure on social media, acknowledges how communitarian narratives inherited are used by social media companies to encourage users to share more data and as counternarratives to conventional concerns about privacy. Likewise, Kennedy (2013) argues that social media platforms position the imperative of sharing within a participatory culture whose objective is community development. In this rhetoric of sharing, Kennedy (2013, p. 132) notes, users are expected to share for the common good of the community: "Good subjects post, update, like, tweet, retweet, and most importantly, *share.*" Social media platforms, some scholars (e.g., John 2013a; Kennedy 2013; Van Dijck 2013) argue, have mobilized the meaning of the word "sharing". Building on Castells (2009), who suggested that today's communication landscape is embedded in a culture of sharing, Kennedy (2013) observes that sharing is the rhetoric of the social web. She suggests that while the term "platform" has been associated with a neutrality principle, as other authors have noted (e.g., Gillespie 2010; Van Dijck 2013), the term "sharing" has positive connotations. Kennedy (2013) finds this association problematic because it hides the real monetization intentions of the use of the term by social media monopolies. Kennedy (2013) argues that the mobilization of the meaning of the term "sharing" has been engineered by social media companies.

John (2013a) looked at how Facebook portrays itself through its communications and found out that Facebook used affective terminology to refer to the act of sharing. He found out that words such as "friend" and "caring" were often associated with sharing practices for the platform to promote its services. Thus, social media platforms have appropriated and mobilized some terms such as "friend", "social", and "sharing", which are part of the culture of engineered sociality. The main feature that promotes the sharing of feelings is the status update feature. Thus, John (2013b) notes, in both Facebook and Twitter status updates sharing means telling; he suggests that users are encouraged to share their feelings with questions such as "What's on your mind?" John (ibid.), drawing on Illouz (2007), finds connections between the positive connotation of sharing on social media and the therapeutic narrative of sharing one's feelings. For instance, in the description of the "Share button", Facebook uses the expression "the people you care about" to refer to the public that your act of sharing is meant for (John 2013b, p. 125). John (ibid.) suggests that the act of sharing is constitutive of social relations, and sharing any kind of content, including one's feelings, has become central in the creation and maintenance of intimate relations.

The design of social media platforms and the visibility of the interaction among members they afford have normalized public exposure with the aim to keep people sharing information, as these platforms use this data for profit. Several scholars (e.g., Miller 2011; John 2013b; Van Dijck 2013; Brake 2014) point out that social media have normalized public disclosure, so the increasing public exposure through different platforms is changing existing social norms and the boundaries between the public and the private. In this context, Van Dijck (2013) argues that social media is a public realm where norms are shaped. She suggests that the power of norms in social interaction is more influential than the power of law, and the quick evolution of the norms for "sharing" private information in the context of online interaction is a good example. Thus, in line with John's (2013a) argument, Van Dijck (2013) believes that social media platforms have deliberately participated in the change of social norms to foster users to disclose more personal information in order to monetize users' information by selling it to advertisers. She analyses how Mark Zuckerberg claimed in 2010 in an interview for *Time* magazine that the objective of Facebook was to create a platform where "the default is social" in order to "make the world more open and connected" (Van Dijck 2013, p. 45). For Van Dijck (2013, p. 45–46), Facebook's "radical transparency" philosophy is encapsulated through the use of the word "sharing": "The values of openness and connectedness are quintessentially reflected in the word favoured most by Facebook's executives: *sharing*." This principle of radical transparency, coined by Anderson (2006) in reference to the openness in the disclosure and management of data by organizations, is useful to understand this shift towards a more open and transparent society. In this context, transparency is understood as being beneficial for personal relations in the sense that it helps to eliminate deceptive and antisocial behaviour. Thus, continues Van Dijck (2013, p. 46), this new imperative of sharing by default has also mobilized the meaning of privacy as something negative, which implies "opacity, nontransparency, and secrecy". She disagrees with Mark Zuckerberg's statement about privacy being an "evolving norm" (ibid.) by arguing that it is actually the concept of sharing which is evolving.

Facebook is the social media platform that has been claimed to be mainly responsible for the evolution of the concept of sharing. Nevertheless, Facebook has never revealed that their intention was to create an attractive platform to facilitate sociability in order to generate profit from users' data, argues Van Dijck (2013), nor have they explained openly how they were actually monetizing the impressive traffic that the site supports. Despite claims made by social media CEOs against monetary gain being the main objective of their service, widely discussed by Dror (2013) in his article "'We Are Not Here for the Money': Founders' Manifestos", some scholars (e.g., John 2013b; Kennedy 2013; Van Dijck 2013; Brake 2014) suggest the contrary. Kennedy (2013) points out that the underlying objective in the imperative of sharing is the generation of profit. In the next section, I continue the analysis of Web 2.0 technologies to discuss the tensions between participatory culture and commodification that operate in social media interaction.

5.3   SOCIAL MEDIA DYNAMICS: BETWEEN EMPOWERMENT AND COMMODIFICATION

In recent years an extensive body of literature has discussed the potentialities for empowerment through the use of Web 2.0 technologies. The main claims are that they increase agency, creativity, and participation. On the other hand, some authors criticize the commercial turn that the Internet experienced in the last decades, and Web 2.0 companies for commoditizing users' data and their lack of transparency in this process. As the focus of my research is intimacy practices, I discuss the commodification of intimacy and personal life both by users and by social media companies. I address how Web 2.0 is approached from three different perspectives: (1) a tool which empowers users by allowing them to do things together; (2) a capitalist system that fosters the commodification of personal relationships and intimacy; and (3) a technology which both empowers users and takes advantage of their personal data for profit, the perspective where I locate myself.

First, I review the benefits of the use of social media. Web 2.0 technologies have been claimed to be empowering for their users insofar as they allow and facilitate lower communication costs (e.g., Curran 2012), collaboration (e.g., Barbrook 1998; Jenkins 2006; Jenkins et al. 2013), democracy (e.g., Coleman and Kaposi 2009; Papacharissi 2010), social capital (e.g., Wellman et al. 2003; Ellison et al. 2011), and intimacy (e.g., Baym 2010; Chambers 2013; Jamieson 2013; boyd 2014). Barbrook (1998) was one of the first authors to refer to the participatory ethos of the social web, which he suggested was embedded in the gift culture. Barbrook (ibid.) highlighted how these ethics come from the counter-culture movements of May 1968. Later, other authors discussed how the collaboration through the Internet could lead to a wide enhanced knowledge, what Lévy (2001, p. 111) labels "collective intelligence". The Wikipedia would be a good example of this phenomenon. Jenkins (2006) also acknowledged the possibilities of collaboration through online interaction; in particular, he focused his attention on fan cultures. Jenkins (2006, p. 3) coined the term "participatory culture" to describe cultural production by fans. On the other hand, some authors (e.g., Coleman and Kaposi 2009; Papacharissi 2010) point to the democratic potentials of Web 2.0, as they see the online environments as the new public sphere, because on social media platforms anyone can post comments and debate.

Another concept closely interrelated to participation on social media is social capital, which relates to the benefits from personal associations (Putman 2001). In this regard, Wellman et al. (2003) found that online interaction increased social capital. Vitak et al. (2011) conducted a study to understand how users perceived gaining social capital through Facebook interaction. Following Putman (2001), Vitak et al. (ibid.) differentiate between bonding social capital (close relationships, which provide help and emotional support) and bridging social capital (weak ties, which may facilitate useful novel information such as finding a job). They concluded that Facebook played an accrual role in developing bonding social capital, especially when the close relationships were situated in distant locations.

Second, I address the issue of commodification of data and intimate relationships in social media contexts. Hesmondhalgh (2013, p. 69) explains that "commodification involves transforming objects and services into commodities", namely, things that can be exchanged and sold. As Hesmondhalgh (2013) observes, the study of the issue of commodification raises questions about what kind of information can be traded. Most societies believe certain domains should be protected from market intervention, which include one's personal life, religion, and political views. It seems that both social media companies and users engage in the commodification of users' private lives, relationships, and personal data.

Social media business models range from paid services to *freemium* models[1] to online advertising. Overall, the most common way of monetize Web traffic is through the commodification of users' data to provide them tailored advertisements or share this data with third parties. As Brake (2014) observes, most social media platforms' revenue comes from customized advertising, whose value depends mainly on the ability to target users with online advertising based on their information. Shepherd (2014) explains that in addition to the traditional way of audience commodification of mass media, advertising takes a new dimension in social media contexts because marketers can gather users' personal and behavioural information. From a critical political economy approach and drawing attention to the issue of commodification, some authors (e.g., Andrejevic 2010; Gillespie 2010; Couldry 2012; Basset 2013; Gehl 2013, 2014; Van Dijck 2013; Fuchs 2014) argue that online customized advertising is a mechanism by which Internet companies commoditize users. In order to

---

[1] *Freemium* business models include a basic service for free, as well as paid premium options (Doerr et al. 2010).

participate in social media services, users must create an account and disclose certain kinds of personal information such as gender, date of birth, and location, which can then be used by companies in marketing campaigns. Gehl (2014, p. 16) explains that social media companies gather more personal information such as "user names, images, personal interests, wishes, likes and dislikes", which are used to customize advertisements and segment audiences. As Couldry (2012) notes, the focus in today's media environment is on the identification of niche audiences catalogued as high-value consumers via continuous online tracking.

In this sense, Gillespie (2010) explains that commercial advertising does not fit with the collaborative and communitarian network culture ethos discussed earlier. Moreover, he highlights that user-generated content is being used to generate traffic to sites where users do not receive any revenue in return. By the same token, Andrejevic (2010) notes that users' immaterial labour generates value for social media companies, although these users may enjoy in the process. Andrejevic (2010, p. 82) argues that "online forms of co-creation complicate standard critiques of exploitation", in the sense that users freely upload content on social media without any kind of coercion, although this has been discussed in terms of peer pressure to participate in the network and a social need for connectivity. Thus, users obtain connectivity, social capital, and reputation management in exchange for their personal and behavioural data. As Basset (2013) observes, personal data is the currency for participating in social media.

By placing emphasis on the affective nature of social media interaction, some scholars have discussed the production of value under different names: free labour (Terranova 2000), playbour (Kücklich 2005), and affective labour (Gehl 2013), depending on the area the analysis is focused on. Gehl (2013) observes that the kind of activities that users perform on social media, such as liking, chatting, friending, or commenting, are usually emotional, affective labour. Drawing on Terranova's (2000, p. 33) concept of "social factory", Andrejevic (2010, p. 90) explains how social media platforms extract value from user sociability: "The social factory puts our pleasure, our communications, our sociability to work, capturing them in order to extract value from them." Likewise, Arvidsson (2006, p. 672) argues that personal relationships "can be subsumed under capital as a source of surplus value" in the context of online dating. Thus, Van Dijck (2013, p. 16) highlights that commoditizing relationships is what social media platforms have discovered as "the golden egg their geese produced".

Illouz (2007) introduces the concept of "emotional capitalism" (2007, p. 60) to explain how intimate life and economy are intertwined and mutually shape each other. Illouz (2007) suggests that we live embedded in an emotional culture based on an ideal of authenticity through the display of intimacy, which generates new intersections of public and private life. In this changing environment, argues Illouz (2007, p. 109), intimate lives are increasingly represented and articulated through social media, reflecting the culture of "emotional capitalism", where "emotions have become entities to be evaluated, inspected, discussed, bargained, quantified and commodified". Using dating sites as a case study, Illouz (2007, p. 36) argues that the management of personal relationships follows the logic of the market: "[R]elationships have been transformed into cognitive objects that can be compared with each other and are susceptible to cost-benefit analyses." Verdú (2005, p. 71) suggests that pervasive consumer society is leading individuals to desire "the consumption of the other". Verdú (ibid.) claims that subjects become objects of desire, giving way to *sobjects*. In the CouchSurfing case, for instance, Bialski (2007) argues that users engage in "emotional tourism", where one does not observe the individual's desire to experience the private, the "house", but a need to experience another human being. Thus, some authors (e.g., Verdú 2005; Bialski 2007; Lardellier 2015) suggest that with the advent of social media, intimacy has become a commodity in itself, and as a result, social media users also engage in the objectification of other users, and even of themselves. Some participants also made reference to the objectification of users in the dating process. Petro (29, Spain) suggested during the interview that Badoo was based on physical beauty, and he explained that he and his friends only talked to users they found attractive because it was the only feature they actually perceived online. Likewise, Cesar (44, Spain) observed: "[I]t usually happens that if you don't like the picture you don't talk to that person." In addition, most Badoo users do not read the text on user profiles. I experienced this during the first phase of the fieldwork when I could see that most users who interacted with me had not read my profile. Ramon (37, Spain) complained about this issue, and he considered that dating services were only a good tool to find a partner for "handsome people" (a group in which he did not include himself). As Illouz (2007) observes, beautiful pictures are key elements for self-promotion in the dating market. This may give the impression that these platforms are a bit superficial and that only good-looking people with sexy pictures are successful on them.

It seems that users also internalize the logics of the market and engage in self-branding and self-commodification. Some scholars (e.g., Arvidsson 2006; Illouz 2007; Heino et al. 2010; Enguix and Ardèvol 2011; Cocks 2015; Lardellier 2015; Lindsay 2015) have analysed how in the online dating environment, users follow the logic of the market to find a partner. In Enguix and Ardèvol's (2011, p. 506) study, one participant compared the dating service to a "meat market", where the interaction was mainly led by the looks. Drawing on Jagger (2001), Lindsay (2015) suggests that the dating industry transforms users into products marketable as daters based on physical attractiveness, which Lardellier (2015) calls "romance marketing". Lardellier (2015) explains how the site AdoptaUnTio (AdoptAGuy) uses the market metaphor to the extreme, as the platform design is a virtual supermarket. In this site, where the women choose who to talk to, men are represented as products to buy. Market metaphors were common when discussing online dating with participants. For example, Raquel (35, Spain) commented that on Badoo you are "on sale".

In generalist social media platforms, such as Facebook or Instagram, a lot of content users share is related to their private lives. As some scholars argue (e.g., Hearn 2008, 2010; Marwick and boyd 2011; Senft 2012; Marwick 2013), users may curate and commoditize this content in order to promote themselves in the network, in order to create value in the "attention economy" (Marwick 2013, p. 143). Hearn (2010) has conducted a critical analysis of the digital reputation economy, by using a historical perspective. Hearn (2010) uses the term "self-branding" to describe how people who are immersed in the celebrity culture disclose intimate information to gather public attention and build reputation. Marwick and boyd (2011), in their empirical study about celebrity culture on Twitter, argue that there are tensions between me-marketing practices and the possibility of creating deeper connections with other users. Marwick and boyd (2011) point out that the practice of commoditizing one's private life is seen as anti-normative. Cocks (2015) notes that the rise of online dating services is often connected to the dominance of capitalism, which extends to their users, who engage in self-marketing strategies. In this study, in order to try to claim attention from other users, some participants explained how they analysed other users' profiles to find tips to enhance their own profiles. As commented earlier, Heino et al. (2010) argue that online daters feel better about themselves as a result of self-branding practices. On the contrary, in my study, some participants expressed frustration with their self-marketing skills, which they deemed responsible for their lack of success—for example, Ramon (37, Spain), who even asked me for tips to improve his profile.

Third, I approach the perspective that considers that social media simultaneously empower users and commoditize users' data. Social media have been claimed to be both empowering and controlling (e.g., Hinton and Hjorth 2013; Jenkins et al. 2013). For instance, Hinton and Hjorth (2013) discuss how social media platforms afford users a certain level of empowerment by allowing them to express themselves and connect with people all around the world, but at the same time, they control users' agency insofar as social media companies gather users' data and use it for profit. Likewise, Jenkins et al. (2013) note that it is important to observe both forces of empowerment and commodification when conducting a critical analysis of social media. The failure to acknowledge this double logic may lead to myopic utopian or dystopian accounts of the social media ecosystem. On the other hand, Hinton and Hjorth (2013) observe how Web 2.0 allows users to become producers of content by disrupting the traditional media production model dominated by a few. Nevertheless, at the same time, they argue Web 2.0 technologies may control users' social lives. In this sense, Jenkins et al. (2013) suggest that despite social media companies receiving profit from users' data, it is necessary to acknowledge that participating in social media services may be meaningful and rewarding for users. Moreover, we cannot assume that users are completely unaware of the logic of commodification inherent in participation on social media services. In fact, as Jenkins et al. (2013) note, users are learning about the workings of social media companies. Thus, users' agency cannot be dismissed. When asking participants whether they would pay to access social media platforms without monitoring, most of them replied that they would not pay or that they would be willing to pay a small fee. Although some participants were concerned about data mining on Facebook, especially by the government, most of them accepted the trade-off of monitoring for connectivity, as the following interview extracts show:

> I've seen in the tablet that it says: "this software can check your data", and you have to accept it, you enter in the game, because at the end of the day social media are tools to keep connected with your friends, so at the end you accept the game. (Raquel, 35, Spain)

In these kinds of things, if it is anonymous I don't mind, because it's marketing and I understand that they have to make money in some way, I
understand the reasons and I even think that it's ok, it has to be a business,
it's like this, and I would never pay, I prefer they use my data than to pay.
(Peter, 34, UK)

There's this myth the Internet is free. Of course it's not free, we pay for it
through being advertised to which I'm okay with that. I don't mind having
banner ads, as long as it's not too intrusive, I accept that and I guess if I'm
going to be advertised to I'd rather I'm offered and told about things that
are of interest to me. (John, 28, UK)

Despite a number of media scholars (e.g., Couldry 2012; Gehl 2013; Van
Dijck 2013) conducting research about the exploitative nature of social
media business models, who mainly claim that users are unaware of the
workings of social media monopolies, in this study, most participants were
aware of how social media political economy worked. However, they considered it a fair trade-off, monitoring their social media activity to target
them with tailored advertisement as exchange to enjoy the service because
the service was "for free". Although most participants considered it a fair
trade-off to be the object of social media monitoring on Facebook, a few
of them also wished they had the possibility of choosing to opt out of
social media monitoring, which could be through a paid option, as in the
case of CouchSurfing, since users who pay for verification do not see
advertising.

5.4   THE MONETIZATION OF INTIMACY: WHO CARES?

Social media business models range from paid services to *freemium* models to customized advertising through users' data mining. In this section,
I examine the different premium services that Badoo and CouchSurfing
charge for. The analysis of my case studies' business models is comple-
mented with adults' perspectives about how they perceive the monetization of intimacy through social media platforms, where most participants
accepted market intervention in the creation of new relationships.

Badoo and CouchSurfing are both based on *freemium* business models.
Badoo offers paid premium services, which can be purchased through

credits or a premium membership (formerly called *superpowers*). Credits[2] allow users to purchase the following services: rise up to first place (in searches), send virtual gifts, ad fun stickers to chats, get featured (top positioning in the home in a given area that lasts five minutes), get their profile shown more, appear more times in "Encounters" (a matching system), chat to five more people in a single day, and appear as "I'm online". Badoo allows individual users to contact up to 15 people per day for free. So using credits to contact five more people is useful, for example, if a user wants to talk to more people on one particular day. In fact, as Cesar (44, Spain) observed, if you pay for credits, it does not mean that you actually talk to 40 people; it means that you have the possibility to try to contact them.

Through their premium service, Badoo offers users to find out who liked their profile, to see who adds them to their favourites, to deliver their messages first, to be able to undo the "No" vote in Encounters, chat to popular users, have their message read first, and visit other users' profiles invisibly. In this subscription service[3] the default setting is that the subscription will be renewed automatically. In fact, Mateo (47, UK) complained because he did not notice that the option of automatic renewal had been automatically checked. He only wanted to pay for the service for one month and he ended up paying for three months because he did not know how to change the option. Lack of trust in the service was identified as a reason to stop using Badoo, as in the case of Mateo, whose distrust led him to decide not to use the service any more. This default setting is a common way to catch users to get them to pay more months than they expected. Unsubscribing from the service is complicated, since the option is hidden. Most participants who had tried *superpowers* commented that premium services were useful to contact popular women. Petro (29, Spain) reported that he tried *superpowers* once because he wanted to talk to some "popular girls". Cesar also explained that *superpowers* were the only way to reach popular women. As Raquel (35, Spain) commented earlier, women receive plenty of messages on Badoo, and *superpowers* allow users to deliver their messages first. Patricia questioned whether the actual

---

[2] Credits can be purchased in different packs, which range from 100 credits for £3 to 2750 credits for £44.99.

[3] There are five different subscriptions types, which range from 1 week for £4.99/week to 6 months for £65,99/month to lifetime for £119,99.

business model of Badoo was providing the company with enough revenue: "If most people use the free version of the site … the website cannot earn a living from four people who pay for the *superpowers*" (Patricia, 31, Spain).

Users can try premium membership for free by sharing their contacts from their email account with Badoo, which gives permission to the platform to send invitations to their contacts to join the network. Marc (39, Spain) reported that he tried *superpowers* for free, but then his contacts received messages from Badoo to join and he did not like it, because he could be perceived as a spammer. The purpose of this practice is to recruit new users, and it actually works. When asking participants about the first time they heard about Badoo, Laura (40, Spain) explained that she joined the platform as a result of receiving this type of message. It is also possible to try premium services when creating a new profile. All participants were aware of the *freemium* business model behind Badoo, and some of them commented that they found Badoo's promotion of its premium services intrusive. There were complaints about Badoo's bad business practices as a source of mistrust (e.g., intrusive and misleading ways of recruiting new users or hidden renovation of monthly subscriptions). Meanwhile, in the case of CouchSurfing, some participants did not have a clear idea whether there was a business model behind the service. For example: "I think (Badoo) it's more business oriented and CouchSurfing is completely free, there is no charge or anything of that sort, so that stands out" (Isaac, 26, UK).

As explained in the previous chapter, Couchsurfing was created in 2004 and developed as a not-for-profit organization run mainly by volunteers until 2011, when it received $7 million from venture capitalists and became a B corporation (Feldman 2012). CouchSurfing received additional funding in 2012, which accounted for a total investment of $22.6 million in the company (Gallagher 2012). Since then, the owners have been experimenting with different ways of monetizing the traffic of the site. From 2015, CouchSurfing has incorporated advertising in the site for users who are not verified, and they also promote the verification system (which costs $25) as another source of revenue. It prevents users from seeing advertising on the site and promises to find them hosts twice as fast. Also, non-verified users can only contact ten maximum hosts per week. However, participants in this study paid for verification when the service was a charity run and supported by users, because they wanted to help to maintain the site. As the ratio of verified users on CouchSurfing is still quite low, and the company did not earn enough revenue from this feature, they incorporated advertising at the beginning of 2015.

CouchSurfing was the site that participants expressed major concerns about its current for-profit-driven business model, since it changed from having charity status to a B corporation. The main issue that participants had with the commercial turn of CouchSurfing was that the hospitality exchange service is based on the altruism of its users; the service was developed by the community and now a few people (founders and venture capitalists) aim to gain money from couchsurfers' hospitality. CouchSurfing is based on the "gift economy" (e.g., Barbrook 1998), where people do things for one another, in the spirit of building something between them, rather than a strict quid pro quo. In fact, most participants considered "saving money" to be a wrong motivation for choosing to participate in the service, as they considered it not to be part of the altruistic spirit of CouchSurfing. Thus, most participants did not consider it ethical for people to use CouchSurfing to save money or to earn money out of altruistic hospitality. When altruism and affective relationships become commoditized by economic interests, participants felt that they were exploited. CouchSurfing was founded in San Francisco, which was the main hub for the emergence of virtual communities in the 1980s based on communitarian and hippie values, as we saw in Chap. 1. Thus, the CouchSurfing ethos is rooted in free exchange and communitarian culture, which is incompatible with market intervention. That is the reason why long-term CouchSurfing participants expressed their disapproval of the commercial turn the site has taken. The affective labour was made more visible when the site changed from an open-source platform to a commercial one, compared to sites such as Facebook, which was privately owned from its inception. On the other hand, John (28, UK) was one of the few users in favour of CouchSurfing being for profit. In fact, what John found problematic was that CouchSurfing did not have a clear business model, as he thought that the company needed money to improve the user experience they offered through their mobile app.

On the other hand, apart from the debate about the monetization of personal relationships by social media companies, participants also discussed about the morality of the intervention of money in the creation of new relationships. Drawing on the notion that the real creator of value in online environments is relationships, Arvidsson (2006) argues that this value is so marketable that online platforms can charge access fees. Many online dating platforms charge a small fee to access the platform or particular premium services (e.g., Match, Badoo). Yoder (2014) explains that the industry behind the online dating market has reached a value of $2 billion. Lardellier's (2015) study explores the political economy of dating sites in France. Some of his participants compared the use of online dating to prostitution, since they were paying "to have relationships with a stranger" (Lardellier 2015, p. 2). Intimacy, Zelizer (2009) notes, often appears like a commodity. Zelizer (ibid.) highlights that historically there has been an ongoing interaction between intimacy and economy. For instance, she explains that sexual relationships often include a transfer of money, being in the shape of marriage, prostitution, or courtship. In this sense, people engage in categorizations of "good" and "bad" intimacy practices, by drawing moral boundaries. Zelizer (2009) explains that people constantly negotiate intimate ties and economic relations, for example, through gift-giving or economic collaboration within households. Thus, in her view, this is not a new phenomenon. Even if intimacy and economy have long been closely intertwined, and mutually sustaining, social media may make this relationship more visible. Nevertheless, some participants were not comfortable with the idea of paying to meet a potential partner. For instance, Ramon found that it was sad that personal relationships were commoditized. Ramon believed that money should not be involved in the creation of personal relationships:

> There's no way I'm going to pay. [...] Because then it becomes a trade, then it becomes a factory, it becomes totally ridiculous for me. [...] I think it's sad and sick that people need to pay to meet somebody. It's really sad. (Ramon, 37, Spain)

Ramon's reference to the intervention of money in the creation of personal relationships as "a factory" links with Terranova's (2000, p. 33) concept of the "social factory", where value is extracted from pleasurable activities such as communication and sociability. However, Ramon contradicted himself because, although he claimed that he would not pay for meeting potential partners, he also stated that it would be a good investment in the case of a positive outcome. Ramon considered that dating sites would be worth paying for if they were more effective.

The fact that the basic service is free was the main motivation for most adults to join Badoo, in the sense of saving money, not because they considered market intervention in the creation of new relationships as unethical. In fact, some participants affirmed that they would pay for online dating services if they had more disposable income. Most participants decided to use Badoo because it was "for free" (despite their personal data being monitored), although they reported not being very successful in the platform. Conversely, Cesar (44, Spain), who often paid for premium services, reported to be very successful in using the platform, in the sense of finding many dates and one-night stands, and he had also found a long-term relationship through Badoo. He valued the service because it made it easier and more comfortable to flirt with people from home, rather than having to go out, and he considered paying to meet people part of the materialistic society we live in: "Obviously we live in a materialistic society, capitalist society, so it's part of it." The market intervention in the creation of new relationships may be interpreted as an unethical commercialization of intimacy, as Ramon opined. However, paying to use social media, especially dating sites, as observed by Cocks (2015), is not so different to buying the newspaper to read the lonely hearts ads section in the past, or to pay a marriage agency in order to find a partner.

5.5   Conclusions

In this chapter, I have analysed the workings of social media platforms, covering social, philosophical, technical, and economic factors that create and encourage a culture of constant connectivity. The political economy of social media is an important factor that determines the design of social media platforms' architecture and the kind of sociability that is fostered within them. Moreover, the commodification of sociality and intimacy is emerging as a new business model. The lack of transparency and the way these sites gather and trade users' information are problematic. However, it is important to acknowledge users' agency when interacting through social media, and the benefits that they receive by participating in the service and in self-branding, including the potential for collaboration, social capital, democracy, and intimacy.

In relation to social media business models, participants expressed their preference for free options with customized advertising, rather than paying a fee. Although advertising in CouchSurfing appeared after my fieldwork was completed, and the verification option prevents users from seeing the advertising, I am unconvinced that users would choose this option to avoid advertising. In general, most participants accepted the trade-off of data mining to serve them customized advertising. In the case of CouchSurfing, participants expressed concerns about the commercial turn the platform had experienced, since they believed they had contributed to the value of the service with their altruistic hospitality, and they did not find it fair that "some people" got money out of it. Thus, on social media a double logic of empowerment and commodification operates: users enjoy a communication tool to create and maintain personal relationships, but at the same time, their affective labour is commoditized in "one way or another".

Market intervention in the creation of new relationships is not a new phenomenon, which might be the reason why there were few participants who found it problematic. Despite people continuously drawing moral boundaries for improper uses of intimacy, market intervention in the creation of intimate relationships has been largely present in society (Zelizer 2009). The findings suggest that what is deemed more problematic is social media companies' bad practices: lack of transparency about the workings of data mining, misleading techniques to get more users, assuring that the platform will never have advertising and including it later on, hiding monthly renewals by default in premium services' payment options, and so on. Therefore, as Jenkins et al. (2013) note, the problem is not the presence of business models, but the bad practices within them. In the next chapter, I analyse what kinds of relationships participants create and develop through Badoo and CouchSurfing, and the different issues that arise from interacting with strangers through these platforms.

References

Anderson, C. (2006, November 26). In praise of radical transparency. *The long tail.* http://www.longtail.com/the_long_tail/2006/11/in_praise_of_ra.html. Date Accessed 25 Nov 2015.

Andrejevic, M. (2010). Social network exploitation. In Z. Papacharissi (Ed.), *Networked self: Identity, community, and culture on social network sites* (pp. 82–102). New York: Routledge.

Arvidsson, A. (2006). "Quality singles": Internet dating and the work of fantasy. *New Media & Society, 8*(4), 671–690.

Barbrook, R. (1998). The hi-tech gift economy. *First Monday, 3*(12), http://journals.uic.edu/ojs/index.php/fm/article/view/631/552. Date Accessed 10 Oct 2013.

Basset, C. (2013). Silence, Delirium, Lies? In G. Lovink & M. Rasch (Eds.), *Unlike us reader: Social media monopolies and their alternatives* (pp. 146–158). Amsterdam: Institute of Network Cultures.

Baym, N. K. (2010). *Personal connection in the digital age*. Cambridge: Polity Press.

Bialski, P. (2007). *Intimate tourism: Friendships in a state of mobility—The case of the online hospitality network*. M.A. thesis, University of Warsaw.

boyd, d. (2014). *It's complicated: The social lives of networked teens*. New Haven: Yale University Press.

Brake, D. R. (2014). *Sharing our lives online: Risks and exposure in social media*. London: Palgrave Macmillan.

Castells, M. (2009). *Communication power*. Oxford: Oxford University Press.

Chambers, D. (2013). *Social media and personal relationships: Online intimacies and networked friendship*. Basingstoke: Palgrave Macmillan.

Cocks, H. G. (2015). The pre-history of print and online dating, c. 1690–1990. In I. A. Degim, J. Johnson, & T. Fu (Eds.), *Online courtship: Interpersonal interactions across borders* (pp. 17–28). Amsterdam: Institute of Network Cultures.

Coleman, S., & Kaposi, I. (2009). A study of e-participation projects in third-wave democracies. *International Journal of Electronic Governance, 2*(4), 302–327.

Couldry, N. (2012). *Media, society, world: Social theory and digital media practice*. Cambridge: Polity Press.

Curran, J. (2012). Rethinking Internet history. In J. Curran, N. Fenton, & D. Freedman (Eds.), *Misunderstanding the Internet* (pp. 3–33). London: Routledge.

Doerr, J., Benlian, A., Vetter, J., & Hess, T. (2010). Pricing of content services: An empirical investigation of music as a service. *Sustainable e-business Management, 58*, 13–24.

Dror, Y. (2013). "We are not here for the money": Founders' manifestos. *New Media & Society, 17*(4), 540–555.

Ellison, N. B., Vitak, J., Steinfield, C., Gray, R., & Lampe, C. (2011). Negotiation privacy concerns and social capital needs in a social media environment. In S. Trepte & L. Reinecke (Eds.), *Privacy online: Perspective on privacy and self-disclosure on the social web* (pp. 19–32). New York: Springer.

Enguix, B., & Ardèvol, E. (2011). Enacting bodies: Online dating and new media practices. In K. Ross (Ed.), *The handbook of gender, sex and media* (pp. 502–515). Oxford: Wiley-Blackwell.

Feldman, Z. (2012). Beyond freedom and oppression: Social media, refusal and the politics of participation. In: IR 13.0 Conference of the AoIR, 18/21 October 2012, Salford. http://spir.aoir.org/index.php/spir/article/view-File/6/pdf. Accessed 18 Feb 2015.

Fuchs, C. (2014). *Social media: A critical introduction*. London: Sage Publications.

Gallagher, B. (2012). CouchSurfing rises $15 million series B from general catalyst partners, Menlo ventures, others. *TechCrunch*. http://techcrunch.

com/2012/08/22/couchsurfing-raises-15-million-series-b-from-general-catalyst-partners-others/. Date Accessed 19 Feb 2015.

Gehl, R. W. (2013). "Why I left Facebook": Stubbornly refusing to not exist even after opting out of Mark Zuckerberg's social graph. In G. Lovink & M. Rasch (Eds.), *Unlike us reader: Social media monopolies and their alternatives* (pp. 220–238). Amsterdam: Institute of Network Cultures.

Gehl, R. W. (2014). *Reverse engineering social media: Software, culture, and political economy in new media capitalism.* Philadelphia: Temple University Press.

Gillespie, T. (2010). The politics of "platforms". *New Media & Society, 12*(3), 347–364.

Hearn, A. (2008). "Meat, mask, burden": Probing the contours of the branded "self". *Journal of Consumer Culture, 8*(2), 197–217.

Hearn, A. (2010). Structuring feeling: Web 2.0, online ranking and rating, and the digital "reputation" economy. *Ephemera, 10*(3/4), 421–438.

Heino, R. D., Ellison, N. B., & Gibbs, J. L. (2010). Relationshopping: Investigating the market metaphor in online dating. *Journal of Social and Personal Relationships, 27*(4), 427–447.

Hesmondhalgh, D. (2013). *The cultural industries* (3rd ed.). London: Sage Publications.

Hinton, S., & Hjorth, L. (2013). *Understanding social media.* London: Sage Publications.

Illouz, E. (2007). *Cold intimacies: The making of emotional capitalism.* Cambridge: Polity Press.

Jagger, E. (2001). Marketing Molly and Melville: Dating in a postmodern, consumer society. *Sociology, 35*(1), 39–57.

Jamieson, L. (2013). Personal relationships, intimacy and the self in a mediated and global digital age. In K. Orton-Johnson & N. Prior (Eds.), *Digital Sociology* (pp. 13–33). New York: Palgrave Macmillan.

Jenkins, H. (2006). *Convergence culture: Where old and new media collide.* New York: New York University Press.

Jenkins, H., Ford, S., & Green, J. (2013). *Spreadable media: Creating value and meaning in a networked culture.* New York: New York University Press.

John, N. A. (2013a). Sharing and web 2.0: The emergence of a keyword. *New Media & Society, 15*(2), 167–182.

John, N. A. (2013b). The social logics of sharing. *The Communication Review, 16*(3), 113–131.

Kennedy, J. (2013). Rhetorics of sharing: Data, imagination, and desire. In G. Lovink & M. Rasch (Eds.), *Unlike us reader: Social media monopolies and their alternatives* (pp. 127–136). Amsterdam: Institute of Network Cultures.

Kücklich, J. (2005). Precarious playbour: Modders and the digital games industry. *Fibreculture, 5.* http://five.fibreculturejournal.org/fcj-025-precarious-playbour-modders-and-the-digital-games-industry/. Date Accessed 10 Oct 2013.

Lardellier, P. (2015). Liberalism conquering love: Reports and reflections on mass romantic and sexual consumption in the Internet age. In I. A. Degim, J. Johnson, & T. Fu (Eds.), *Online courtship: Interpersonal interactions across borders* (pp. 96–105). Amsterdam: Institute of Network Cultures.

Lévy, P. (2001). *Cyberculture*. Minneapolis: University of Minnesota Press.

Lindsay, M. (2015). Performative acts of gender in online dating: An auto-ethnography comparing sites. In I. A. Degim, J. Johnson, & T. Fu (Eds.), *Online courtship: Interpersonal interactions across borders* (pp. 242–261). Amsterdam: Institute of Network Cultures.

Marwick, A. E. (2013). *Status update: Celebrity, publicity, and branding in the social media age.* New Haven: Yale University Press.

Marwick, A. E., & boyd, d. (2011). I tweet honestly, I tweet passionately. Twitter users, context collapse, and the imagined audience. *New Media & Society, 13*(1), 114–133.

Miller, D. (2011). *Tales from Facebook.* Cambridge, MA: Polity Press.

O'Reilly, T. (2005). *What is web 2.0? Design patterns and business models for the next generation of software.* O'Reilly Media, Inc. 30 September. http://www.oreilly.com/pub/a//web2/archive/what-is-web-20.html, Date Accessed 13 July 2014.

Papacharissi, Z. (2010). *A private sphere: Democracy in a digital age.* Cambridge, MA: Polity Press.

Putman, R. (2001). *Bowling alone: The collapse and revival of american community.* New York: Simon and Schister Ltd.

Senft, T. M. (2012). Microcelebrity and the branded self. In J. Burgess & A. Bruns (Eds.), *Blackwell companion to new media dynamics* (pp. 346–654). Oxford: Blackwell.

Shepherd, T. (2014). Gendering the commodity audience in social media. In L. Steiner, L. McLaughlin, & C. Carte (Eds.), *The Routledge companion to media and gender.* New York: Routledge.

Terranova, T. (2000). Free labor: Producing culture for the digital economy. *Social Text, 18*(2), 33–58.

Van Dijck, J. (2013). *The culture of connectivity: A critical history of social media.* Oxford: Oxford University Press.

Van Dijck, J., & Nieborg, D. (2009). Wikinomics and its discontents: A critical analysis of web 2.0 business manifestos. *New Media & Society, 11*(5), 855–874.

Verdú, V. (2005). *Yo y tú, objetos de lujo: El personismo: la primera revolución cultural del siglo XXI.* Barcelona: Random House Mandadori.

Vitak, J., Ellison, N. B., & Steinfield, C. (2011). The ties that bond: Re-examining the relationship between Facebook use and bonding social capital. In *System sciences (HICSS), 4/7 January, Kauai, HI* (pp. 1–10). Kauai: IEEE.

Wellman, B., Quan-Haase, A., Boase, J., Chen, W., Hampton, K. N., & Díaz de Isla Gómez, I. (2003). The social affordances of the Internet for networked

individualism. *Journal of Computer-Mediated Communication, 8*(3). http://
onlinelibrary.wiley.com/doi/10.1111/j.1083-6101.2003.tb00216.x/full.
Date Accessed 5 June 2012.

Yoder, S. (2014). How online dating became a $2 billion industry. *Fiscal Times.*
http://www.thefiscaltimes.com/Articles/2014/02/14/Valentines-Day-
2014-How-Online-Dating-Became-2-Billion-Industry.   Date   Accessed   5
December 2015.

Zelizer, V. A. (2009). *The purchase of intimacy.* Princeton: Princeton University
Press.

CHAPTER 6

Meeting People Online

Abstract There are a number of social media services for meeting new people online. In particular, this chapter is focused on Badoo (dating/hook-up platform) and CouchSurfing (hospitality exchange/meet-up platform). Other dating sites were incorporated in the analysis since participants also used these services. In this chapter, the importance of developing trust to create new relationships through social media and issues related to authenticity and social stigma are covered. Then, different kinds of safety issues that users may face when meeting people online, which range from online harassment to robbery to sexual harassment, are addressed. This is followed by a discussion about the reproduction of gender roles through social media. Finally, the chapter presents a debate about the quality of Internet-initiated relationships.

Keywords Badoo • CouchSurfing • Intimacy • New relationships • Online dating • Trust

6.1 INTRODUCTION

Social media platforms are mainly used to maintain ongoing relationships or keep in contact with acquaintances. Nevertheless, there are specific platforms to meet new people online, which range from dating sites to hospitality exchange networks to meet-up services. Although there are people who also create new relationships through Facebook, most

© The Author(s) 2018   103
C. Miguel, *Personal Relationships and Intimacy in the Age of Social Media*, https://doi.org/10.1007/978-3-030-02062-0_6

participants in this study used Facebook mainly to maintain ongoing relationships. For this reason, in this chapter, I focus on Badoo and CouchSurfing experiences, as discussed by participants during the interviews. Both Badoo and CouchSurfing platforms are designed to create personal relationships in which people usually move the interaction offline and meet face-to-face. As some authors observe (e.g., Chambers 2006; boyd 2010b), despite Internet-initiated relationships having the potential to develop into long-term romantic relationships or friendships, they are usually considered superficial and transient. In fact, to investigate this topic was one of the main motivations I initially had to study intimate relationships that had originated via social media. In the last section, I explore whether users think that the relationships they started online are more superficial than the relationships that they created in other places. First, I address how participants deal with trust issues, social stigma, and safety concerns when participating in social media to meet new people. Moreover, I show how patriarchal gender roles are often reproduced online.

6.2   Trust, Deception, and Social Stigma

Most people join social media services in order to keep in contact with existing relationships, but some social media platforms facilitate making new friends or finding partners. The Internet allows users to overcome physical barriers; however, there are a lot of people who are not motivated to interact with strangers (boyd 2010a). In the context of online interaction with strangers, where users seek to create new relationships, the generation of trust is very important. To be intimate, Marar (2012, p. 77) argues, requires that "we are confident enough to confide our confidences to a confidant: 'for your eyes only'". Intimate relationships, as Zelizer (2009) notes, depend on a degree of trust. Trust fosters intimate self-disclosure, and therefore, involves positive and negative implications for the trustors. Giddens (1992) argues that trust and accountability are closely tied together and they need to be reciprocal to create long-lasting intimate relationships. Lack of trust had a negative impact on the engagement in intimacy practices through social media. For example:

> I can't feel really intimate, or let's say confident, when I'm having a kind of relationship with people only by Internet or social media. I can't call them my friends or something like this but only if I know somebody in person

then sometimes it is something like friendship or not, but only if I know this person from my "real life". I just don't trust the Internet personally for this. (Noelia, 25, UK)

It's like until you actually meet them you don't know whether it's actually genuine they say they are. So you always have to be a little bit guarded with that. (Gary, 43, UK)

In fact, a major concern, in particular on Badoo, was related to the authenticity of the users. This is a theme that has been widely investigated in Internet scholarship. Several scholars (e.g., Hall et al. 2010; Heino et al. 2010; Gibbs et al. 2011) have studied deception in the context of online dating. The extreme case of deception online is called "catfishing" and it refers to the misleading practice of impersonating other people on online platforms. Rasmussen (2014) has analysed how audiences perceive online dating through the MTV programme *Catfish*. This programme addresses people's motivations to participate in online dating and why some users engage in deceptive practices in order to achieve romantic goals by creating fake profiles, mainly on Facebook. Although no participant reported to have been "catfished", a couple of participants explained that they had chatted with girls who had fake pictures in their profiles on Badoo. For example, Cesar (44, Spain) reported to be talking to a girl who was using the pictures of a Russian model. They even talked about this, and she was happy that he still wanted to continue talking to her despite knowing she was not the girl in the pictures. In addition, a common authenticity issue was related to users uploading pictures where they were much younger. Mateo (47, UK) had a date with a woman who in her profile had uploaded photos where she was ten years younger, which made him feel very disappointed when they met in person. Heino et al. (2010), in their research about online dating, found similar deceptive practices. Likewise, Hall et al. (2010) found that women under 50 are more likely to misrepresent their age. Thus, we can observe deceptive practices in online dating, mainly related to users uploading pictures of themselves when they were much younger. Some participants noted that Badoo users engaged in this practice in order to be contacted by more people because one's physical appearance is hugely important on dating sites, as we observed in the previous chapter. For this reason, after ten years of using the hook-up site AdultFriendFinder, Oscar (41, UK) has learnt to verify the identity of his potential encounters through different mediums before meeting them face-to-face:

> There is literally every scenario that you could imagine, you will find on AdultFriendFinder. And you've got to find your own ways to navigate that, so if I'm going to meet somebody, OK, we need to Skype, you need to call me and I need to know that you're genuine. (Oscar, 41, UK)

Authenticity issues arise when interacting through dating/hook-up sites, which create problems for initiating new relationships. For this reason, verification and reputation systems are useful to foster trusting relationships among users. In the case of Badoo, the verification of users' identity with other social media presence may act as a guarantee.

Some scholars (e.g., Ellison et al. 2006; Hearn 2008; Baym 2010; Marwick 2013) state that users engage in impression management through social media, the so-called self-branding (Hearn 2008), to present themselves positively and attractively. For some users, the practice of self-branding may be perceived as performance and lacking of authenticity. On the other hand, if we offer different presentations of the self to address different audiences in the same context, Lambert (2013) argues, part of the audience may consider unauthentic a particular "version" of the self that we are displaying. In this sense, Lambert (2013) suggests that accurate self-disclosure appears as the "desirable happening" (emphasis added) in order to foster the development of intimacy. Lambert (ibid.) argues that authenticity may be seen as the desirable characteristic of self-presentation in order to build intimacy, but he also identifies tensions between authenticity and performance in different social contexts. Therefore, he suggests that in the context of social media, it would be useful to avoid linking the concept of intimacy with the presentation of an authentic self because the concept of authenticity is contextual.

In addition, despite online dating becoming an everyday practice, there is still a certain stigma. Among my interviewees, Patricia commented that most people believed that those who interact with strangers online only want sex: "It's a bit bad seen. If you talk through the web they think that you want sex" (Patricia, 31, Spain). In addition, most participants pointed out that people who use social media to create new relationships are considered to be socially awkward or lack the social skills to meet people in another environment, as other studies have shown (e.g., Peter and Valkenburg 2007; boyd 2008). The last Pew Research Center report about online dating found that many people still remain puzzled that someone would want to find a romantic partner online, since 23% of US population agree with the statement that "people who use online dating sites are desperate" (Smith and Anderson 2016). There were still some participants who had a stigma about meeting people online themselves, or who observed this stigma in other users in relation to the use of online dating platforms:

> I have a lot of friends that found a boyfriend online. I don't live in an environment where this practice is stigmatized, but I know other girls who have this very hidden. (Raquel, 35, Spain)

> In a dating site there is a taboo, they tell you: "People around me don't know that I'm in this website", "A friend of mine created my profile", "I'm here but I don't use it very often." [...] "Well, I'm here just to try, I don't believe very much in this, but I'm here", they always need to excuse themselves. (Gemma, 43, Spain)

> I don't want anybody to know that I'm using dating sites. [...] More than for my friends is for myself, I find very frustrated that I'm not able to find someone, because I go to a club and I'm not able to go to talk to a girl. Well, I'm able to, but I'm not successful, and I end up here as a plan B. (Luis, 30, Spain)

In fact, this last participant commented that he felt that he lacked social skills to meet girls face-to-face, and he felt upset with himself for using dating sites as he saw this practice as his last option for finding a partner. It seems that some online daters tend to hide this practice or try to justify for themselves the use of these kinds of sites. Apart from trust issues, most Badoo participants did not add people who they had met on Badoo on Facebook because they did not want their "friends" to know that they were meeting strangers on a dating platform. Few participants said that they added people from Badoo as friends on Facebook, and it was usually after having met offline or because the other person wanted to close their Badoo account.

6.3   Security Concerns

The safe environment that arises online from the lack of immediacy of face-to-face interaction makes social media good for flirting, especially at the beginning of relationships; nevertheless, Chambers (2013) argues, the risks may appear during embodied encounters. Online communication can have the advantage of a certain level of anonymity—especially on dating platforms, where users are encouraged to conceal their full names and information that could identify them to protect themselves (Badoo 2018). At the same time, this level of anonymity fosters misbehaviour as it is difficult to identify offenders. Some female participants reported that they had received unpleasant messages through the chat feature, some of these being sexist comments, a topic that I develop further in the next section. Chambers (2013) argues that a substantial proportion of people who participate in online dating platforms (29%) reported having had negative experiences, mostly related to online harassment. In this study, some participants explained how female users often experience having men aggressively insisting on keeping in contact. For example:

> One day I was contacted by a 40 something years old guy, and I replied to him: "I'm sorry, I don't want to talk to you because I don't see in your profile that we have many things in common, so I'm not interested." But he was insisting a lot. […] Because at the club you tell him: "Go away!" And he has to leave, or you can call security, but on Badoo you can't. Where are you going to say: "this guy is disturbing me?" No, you can't. You can block him, but you already had an unpleasant experience. (Raquel, 35, Spain)

Badoo has taken into account that users may be very disturbed by receiving unwanted messages. For this reason, the platform permits blocking other users in order to avoid receiving unwanted communications. By the same token, Badoo implemented a technical restriction that users cannot contact a person more than twice without receiving a reply. These measures try to protect users from online harassment. Also, verified member can choose to be contacted only by other verified members.

Users may also face identity theft (see Brake 2014) when interacting online. For example, Gemma, a CouchSurfing user, who also is a member of different dating platforms, experienced identity theft on CouchSurfing when someone took pictures from her CouchSurfing profile. It is not clear what the intentions were of the person who created the fake profile with Gemma's pictures. Gemma decided not to go to the police. Instead, she solved this issue through CouchSurfing channels, since she contacted the "Trust & Safety" team, which deleted the fake profile. The possibility also exists of being the subject of a scam or robbery by a stranger met on the Net. There are a number of individuals who use dating platforms to identify vulnerable people and try to take advantage of them, what Whitty and Buchanan (2012, p. 5) have labelled "online dating romance scam". In this study no user experienced any kind of scam; however, Laura reported that she and her flatmates were robbed by a boyfriend she met on Badoo. Laura went to the police and sued her ex-boyfriend. In fact, during the course of the interview in her apartment, the police came to give her the notification of the trial. Petro, who knew about Laura's story, believed that Laura was not the first victim of this criminal. In fact, he thought this was the criminal's *modus vivendi*. In Petro's opinion, these kinds of criminals look for vulnerable people in order to take advantage of them: "He looks for desperate girls, he tells them 'I love you', they fell in love with him, and then …" (Petro, 29, Spain). Despite having had this bad experience, Laura continued using Badoo. She went on dates, but she wanted to "play it safe" this time, so she just wanted to get to know the person well before starting a relationship. Laura explained that one of the men she met on Badoo started to ask her for money by telling her a very sad story. Obviously, after her previous bad experience, Laura did not trust this man and even played with him by telling him that she had won some money in the lottery to see to what extent he was interested in her money.

In the case of CouchSurfing, some participants explained that their relatives or neighbours thought that hosting strangers at home was "weird" and risky. Gemma (43, Spain) reported that people had made her have doubts about hosting through CouchSurfing with their disapproving comments, but she ultimately decided to keep hosting. Other participants commented that their parents were not very happy with the idea, since they had concerns about safety. Scholars have argued that when CouchSurfing members host, they put themselves, as well as their personal belongings, at risk (e.g., Rosen et al. 2011; Bialski 2013). In fact, Raquel (35, Spain) commented that her parents were more concerned about her using CouchSurfing than dating sites. Some participants explained that they felt a bit scared the first times they hosted, but they lost the fear through practice and learning to read profiles, especially references. As Olga put it:

> The first time you host you are like waiting that it is not a "psycho killer" but then you are more relaxed. You learn to read the profiles, to check that the people are more or less serious, if they are an old member or not, if they have experience travelling, and then mostly you read the references. (Olga, 40, Spain)

Both on CouchSurfing and dating sites, female participants have concerns about unwanted sexual advances. In particular, many participants referred to the power imbalance of women being sexually harassed by men who they had met on the platforms. In this sense, participants said that although men could also receive unwanted sexual advances from women, this would not represent a risky scenario. In this study, few participants experienced this kind of harassment themselves or referred to people they knew who experienced an unwanted sexual advance during the hospitality exchange or on a date. Despite the most common practice in CouchSurfing being men hosting women and women hosting men, many participants pointed to the risky scenario of a woman being hosted by a man, and a few of them assumed that female couchsurfers were responsible for protecting themselves from being attacked by men. In this sense, some female participants highlighted that they decided to be hosted only by other women to avoid unwanted sexual advances by men. Some participants pointed to the misconception that some male couchsurfers have the idea that CouchSurfing is like a dating site. Some female couchsurfers reported having received couch requests[1] by males when they had specified on their profiles that they were not hosting at that moment, having received plenty of sexual advances in meetings, or having received messages from men to show them the city where the dating intentions were clear. In relation to sexual assault, some participants referred to the case of a female CouchSurfing user who was raped by her host in Leeds, UK. As Baym (2010) points out, new technologies are always accompanied by moral panics, often including sexual predation. Nevertheless, Baym (ibid.) notes that sexual assaults between strangers remain extremely infrequent in relation to sexual predation within existing relationships, and sexual assaults between people who met online represent a tiny proportion of stranger crimes.

6.4   Reproducing Patriarchal Gender Roles Online

The traditional social convention that dictates that men start flirting with women, while women wait to be approached, could be inverted on social media. Giddens (1992) points out that it is necessary to find a balance of power within personal relationships to avoid intimacy becoming oppres-

---

[1] A couch request is a petition to be hosted by other CouchSurfing users. When looking for a couch, users usually make a search in the city they are visiting and filter in the list the profiles of people who appear as hosting in that moment.

sive. In order to do so, Giddens (1992, p. 94) refers to women's sexual emancipation "no longer harnessed to double standards" as the engine to arrive to the ideal of "the pure relationship", based on the quality of mutual emotional satisfaction. In addition, Giddens (1992, p. 2) coins the term "plastic sexuality" to include non-heteronormative sexual relationships within this sexual emancipation framework. However, some scholars (e.g., Chambers 2013; Jamieson 2013) argue that social media recreate conventional hierarchies of sexuality and gender.

Drawing on Van Doorn and Van Zoonen (2008), Leurs and Ponzanesi (2012) identified three general strands in the literature of gender and the Internet: the utopian, the dystopian, and the in-between perspectives. From a utopian point of view, early cyberfeminist scholars (e.g., Haraway 1997; Plant 1997) argued that the Internet is especially liberating for women. Among other debates around the relationship between humans and technology, Haraway (1997) highlighted that virtual worlds allowed identity play, which would, in turn, help to liberate women from the constraints of a gendered-ruled society. Plant (1997) was one of the first scholars to argue that femininity was the core element of cyberspace. She suggested the medium had the potential for new experiences of intimacy: "[D]igital zone facilitates unprecedented levels of spontaneous affection, intimacy" (Plant 1997, p. 144). Building on Plant, Driscoll (2008) discussed the traditional association between women and intimacy, arguing that women are better able to achieve intimacy through social media, as they are usually more open to sharing feelings.

On the other hand, dystopian views (e.g., Thelwall 2011; Jamieson 2013; Degim and Johnson 2015) show the Internet reproducing existing gender roles. Thelwall (2011) observes that social media interaction usually reflects offline masculinities and femininities. Likewise, Jamieson (2013) suggests that there is little evidence of social media disrupting traditional patriarchal gender roles. As Enguix and Ardèvol (2011) note in their study about dating sites, the socio-technical design reproduces engendered practices, which are interwoven with media practices through bodies and their representations. Degim and Johnson (2015, p. 11) argue that the socio-technological space of social media platforms reproduces patriarchal gender roles, insofar as it "creates an environment of existing beliefs and behaviours that, at times, maintain a hetero-normative hierarchy". In this gendered Internet, Haferkamp et al. (2012, p. 92) suggest that users are aware of the gender norms operating and they "conform to stereotypical gender-specific expectations" to fit in and avoid rejection. In the same vein, Martínez-Lirola (2012) found that patriarchal modes of courtship were reproduced in Badoo.

Finally, scholars (e.g., Wajcman 2010; Leurs and Ponzanesi 2012; Tsatsou 2012; Chambers 2013) do argue that reality lies in an in-between perspective, where gender and the Internet interplay in antagonistic ways. Wajcman (2010, p. 148) argues that "technology as such is neither inherently patriarchal nor unambiguously liberating". In the same vein, Tsatsou (2012) shows that while the Internet opens new spaces for the performance of alternative sexualities, it also supports the "re-masculinization" of gender relationships. Likewise, Chambers (2013) acknowledges the potentiality that social media offer to interact in a safe space where traditional gender inequalities could be overcome, and where both men and women could experiment with new ways to relate to each other. Nevertheless, Chambers (ibid.) observes, people mainly reproduce traditional gender roles online. Giddens (1992) points out that in the postmodern era intimacy has become more flexible and elective. Following Giddens (1992), Chambers (2013) suggests that the innumerable opportunities that social media offer to interact with a broad range of strangers would be an ideal tool to experience more fluid intimacy practices; however, most participants seem to be very traditional in their patterns of interaction. I position my research in this in-between perspective, since I recognize how social media platforms can empower users by helping them to experiment with their sexualities, and create and maintain personal relationships, while this process is still embedded in traditional patriarchal structures, which constrain the potential liberating aspect of social media interaction.

One of the participants who used Badoo to explore her sexual orientation was Sandra (39, UK). Sandra, who is a divorced woman with two children, started to use Badoo to experiment with her feelings towards other women. In this sense, as Chambers (2006) notes, the fluidity of sexual identity can be explored through the interaction with strangers online; nevertheless, in this study the majority of the practices were heteronormative and followed gendered scripts. Most participants agreed that men usually started the conversations in Badoo and considered this "normal". Some participants even implied that if women started the conversation it was because they were desperate. A repeated expression by male participants was "we are the hunters"; it seems that they were trying to look for biological justification to perpetuate traditional courtship conventions. Other participants pointed to the larger numbers of men than women on Badoo in order to justify why men usually start the conversation, in reference to a kind of law of "supply and demand" operating in the platform. On Badoo there are around double the number of males compared to females (Alexa 2018), although some male participants speculated that the difference was bigger because they did not receive responses from women. In the study conducted by Jacobs (2009, p. 2) about AdultFriendFinder, females were found to receive massive amounts of requests from males, while male users may be "starving for a reply for weeks on end". Similarly, I have found that on Badoo, women also receive plenty of messages, while men received few responses. In fact, some female participants made reference to the large number of messages they receive every time they logged in Badoo as the reason why they did not feel the need to actively search for men:

> Because you (as a woman) enter in Badoo and its like "come to me", you know. [...] I don't have to do anything. On the other hand, men have to start to send messages, messages, and if they are lucky some women will answer. (Ana, 35, UK)

Thus, female participants usually selected among the male users who contacted them, and just replied to those that they considered interesting, but they rarely searched for men. In this sense, female users can exercise certain power over male users, since it is hard for men to find a date through Badoo. By the same token, some participants observed that women have more opportunities than men to find a date through Badoo.

The dating site AdoptaUnTio (AdoptAGuy) tries to reverse this dynamic, mainly to make the search for a date/hook-up more comfortable for the women. In this site, men can claim attention from five women a day through "spells" and women may accept or decline the invitation to talk to them. A female user, on the other hand, can talk to male users at any time, and she can put male users in her "shopping basket", which means that she finds them interesting and they can talk to her. There is also the possibility to book a man for 24 hours (an option that the male user has to accept), which means that this user cannot talk to other users during one day. Luis (31, Spain) used this dating platform and he commented that it was more comfortable that women have to give the first step in the conversation, so he just talked to the women who were interested in talking to him. I used AdoptaUnTio for a couple of months, and although it is true that it gives more power to women, I could feel that similar gender roles patterns were reproduced, since I was approached by a large amount of men every day through spells, and then I had to select who to talk to, almost the same as on Badoo. In addition, I could find a lot of Badoo users in AdoptaUnTio as well, coming back to the idea discussed earlier in this chapter that people who use social media to meet new people participate in a number of different social media services.

In the case of Badoo, most female participants were not very happy with the outcome of their interactions in the platform. It seems as though one of the reasons why women do not find what they are looking for on Badoo might be that male and female users have different expectations for the platform. Although most participants agreed that Badoo was mainly targeted as a platform to look for sex, both male and female users believed that women who participated in the site were looking for a relationship, while men were only looking for sex:

On Badoo I look for some interesting guy, not just sex. (Raquel, 35, Spain)

I think that most of men are there just for sex, and other websites are maybe more catered to that, but I don't know why. I don't think that women are there just for sex, I think that they look for more than that. [...] Usually women are more self-guarded; I don't think that they are many women in Badoo looking for sex, unfortunately. (Gary, 43, UK)

In order to navigate this problematic scenario where different expectations collide, some participants explained that male users tend to lie about their objective of participating in the site in order to try to arrange a first date, which makes the initial typical question "What are you looking for?" useless. On the other hand, when men are sexually explicit, women who are looking for a relationship may feel uncomfortable with these kinds of communications. In spite of physical safety issues that women may avoid when interacting online, they can also face some kind of verbal harassment, as we saw in the last section. In this sense, some female participants also explained how male Badoo users talked to them in a very sexually nasty way that they disliked:

The worse is the creeps that pester you on here with dirty rude remarks towards you that's just annoying [...] I can't think of any specific but rude like would like to fuck you, [...] dirty sexual comments. (Sandra, 39, UK)

When men engaged in direct sexual comments some female participants reported feeling offended, and they defined it as a bad experience.
In relation to the disclosure of sexual desire, double sexual standards were
identified, where women who upload very revealing pictures of themselves
were considered to be "sluts". There were some male Badoo users who
claimed that when women upload sexy pictures on Badoo, they *cheapened*
themselves and they would not be interested in contacting "these kinds of
girls" (for a further discussion about visual intimacy on social media, see
Miguel 2016). My research supports previous findings (e.g., Tanenbaum
2015) in suggesting that this patriarchal double sexual standard, about
what kind of women's sexual behaviour is socially acceptable, has been
absolutely reproduced, maintained, and reinforced online. Despite the
apparent possibilities of social media for opening new ways of liberating
both men and women from traditional gender roles (e.g. Chambers
2013), and for making the world more cosmopolitan, the reality is that
patriarchal gender roles are reproduced online. In the next section, I will
explore the kinds of relationships people create online, and whether participants believe that Internet-originated relationships are better, worse, or
of the same quality as relationships created offline.

6.5   TOWARDS EPHEMERAL BUT MEANINGFUL
ASSOCIATIONS

Intimate relationships vary in kind and degree in relation to the amount
and quality of information disclosed, and the level of trust likewise varies
accordingly. In fact, Zelizer (2009) points out, personal relations cannot
be constrained to a binary of strangers and intimates; personal relationships come in many more than two varieties. In this regard, Germann
Molz (2012) argues the social media platforms enable new forms of intimacy and togetherness, and redefine who counts as a "friend" or a
"stranger". Despite the liquidity of personal relationships in contemporary
networked society, Marar (2014) highlights the intrinsic ephemeral character of intimacy per se. Marar (2014) refers to the ephemerality of intimacy, using the term "intimate" to describe both long-term relationships
and one-off encounters between strangers.

   This section explores the tension between how people navigate online/
offline environments and how people make meaning from their transient
(or not) relationships created online. I analyse the dynamics of relation-

ships started through Badoo and CouchSufing, how they develop in embodied encounters, and whether participants believed that these relationships were more superficial and transient than others that they had created in other places. Participants reported different kinds of experiences about meeting people online. In the case of Badoo, despite participants describing the platform as a hook-up and sex-oriented service, most of them claimed that they were looking to meet either people to hang out with or romantic partners. Some of them commented that they had never met anyone face-to-face from Badoo, other participants explained that they had had a few dates, and a few others were actually successful using the platform, since they had found one-night stands and partners.

Although most participants agreed that they would not keep an intimate relationship online only, there were a few participants that had created intimate relationships with people they met on Badoo whom they had never met face-to-face. This is not rare in online dating scenario, as Smith and Anderson (2016) found in their study about online dating in the US, one-third of people who have used online dating have never actually gone on a date with someone they met on these sites. Some participants highlighted that it was hard to move the interaction offline. Sandra (39, UK) reported that she had met her current girlfriend on Badoo a few months before our interview, but they had not met face-to-face yet. They usually talked by phone every day. Her partner gave her different family reasons to avoid the meeting and Sandra was starting to have doubts about the authenticity of her identity. Similarly, Patricia (31, Spain) considered that online relationships were more superficial because you could not be sure that the information that the other users are providing is real. Nevertheless, Patricia, although having not met anyone face to face and having trust concerns, reported to have practiced cybersex through Badoo chat. She also said she had moved the communication to Skype to have a videoconference on some occasions, which is a platform that some users prefer for cybersex. A few other participants commented that other users had invited them to move the conversation to Skype, although most participants reported, as commented earlier, that the most common happening was to move the interaction from Badoo to WhatsApp.

There were diverse opinions about whether relationships created through social media were of the same quality as the relationships built elsewhere. Baym (2010) analysed different studies that compared online and offline relationships, and suggests that only cross-sex friendships started online seem to be of higher quality than those started offline.

Nevertheless, continues Baym (ibid.), long-term studies have shown that there are no meaningful differences between them. In relation to online dating, the study conducted by Smith and Anderson (2016) for the Pew Research Center shows that 5% of US people who are in a marriage or committed relationship say they met their significant other online. In this study, there were some participants who believed that relationships started online were more superficial and less long-lasting than traditional relationships such as best friendships started in childhood. In the case of Badoo, some participants pointed out that they came to that conclusion because they did not find any meaningful relationships through Badoo, but they would think otherwise if they were to find a friend or partner through the site. However, most participants believed that the quality of the relationship was not related to the place of the first contact. They just found social media another venue to connect with people.

Most participants reported that the typical date was going out to have a drink to get to know each other, although a few also said that they went to the cinema or to have dinner with their online dates. In particular, a few of them found the lack of spontaneity problematic. As Chambers (2013, p. 141) puts it: "Conversely, while online romance confirms the late modern ethos of agency, it also suggests that 'romance' is not spontaneous, authentic and passionate process but something necessarily calculated, stage-managed and premeditated." Others complained about the quality of the people who participated on Badoo service in comparison with dating sites such as Meetic or Parship where there was a monthly fee. Nevertheless, in the study about dating sites conducted by Enguix and Ardèvol (2011), where they used Match as a case study (a paid dating service), participants complained about the quality as well. Most participants were using the free version of the site and mentioned that they did not find it efficient, and most participants complained about the "quality" of the people they had encountered in the site, as commented earlier. In this study, there were few participants who had met long-term relationships through Badoo.

Although some participants said that they have found romantic or sexual partners through Badoo or CouchSurfing (in fact, several participants were in a serious relationship with a fellow couchsurfer at the time of the interview), most of them valued the friendships that they created with people they had met through these platforms. In the context of Western society, some scholars (e.g., Chambers 2006; Jamieson et al. 2006) suggest that friendship is increasingly replacing the traditional family-founding couple as the key intimate relationship of adulthood. In this sense, some participants reported that their best experiences of using Badoo had been to create a particular long-lasting friendship that initially started as a potential romantic relationship. Likewise, the main motivation that led participants to use CouchSurfing was to widen their social circle and build new friendships in their area. On both sites, finding "something else" was seen as "a bonus".

Almost half of the participants in this study were expats; for this reason, it is not surprising that they needed to create new personal relationships in their new cities of residence. Among the local participants, some of them also reported that they were not originally from Leeds or Barcelona; therefore, they did not have a big social circle in those cities. Thus, participants also valued augmenting their social life and circle of acquaintances as a result of using CouchSurfing, despite most of those relationships not being very deep. However, some of them used to regularly attend CouchSurfing meetings in their cities and became good friends with other regular local attendees. Travellers also join these meetings, although, as some participants commented, these regular local attendees often create a close circle of friends and it is not easy for the newcomers to enter into the circle. It is also common to find (sexual) partners in these meetings.

In the case of CouchSurfing, keeping in contact after hospitality exchange experiences, or after having met, to visit a city together is not so common. Although the host-guest relationships may seem more intimate insofar as both couchsurfers are sharing the same living space, in this study few participants developed friendships after *surfing* or hosting. Some participants explained that the most likely scenario that happens after the hospitality exchange experience is that they keep in contact online or they lose contact, if they do not live in the same place. Nevertheless, they still valued that ephemeral connection during their stay. It is common that people who are moving to another city request the opportunity to *surf* two or three places while they are finding a place to live. In those cases, if there was a good connection, couchsurfers might keep in contact and even become friends. Despite keeping in contact or not with people they had met through CouchSurfing, participants value the "here and now" experience, especially the "instant social life" when travelling somewhere else.

By the same token, when hosting, some participants pointed to their aim to recreate the same good feeling they had when they were travelling and spending time with local couchsurfers. As they love travelling and meeting local people, they also enjoy showing their city to travellers and helping them have a good experience. Miller (2015) refers to these "here and now" shared experiences as a way of experiencing intimacy and mutual understanding. This "instant social life" and transient experiences that participants make reference to, although fleeting and not very deep, are valued by participants, as they enjoy the company of their new "CouchSurfing friends" for a short period of time, but which is still meaningful for them. As Sara (39, Spain) explains, these ephemeral experiences are not less meaningful for the fact of being short or because you lose contact with the people you share your time with. Miller (2015) makes reference to past romantic relationships as an example of relationships that were meaningful in a particular point of our lives. Likewise, Sara refers to the transient nature of personal relationships in contemporary society. However, she does not take a melancholic point of view like "good old days"; she just does not find the mobility and ephemerality of current personal relationships as problematic. Sara points to a carpe diem philosophy in order to extract the most meaningful experiences in each situation.

6.6   CONCLUSIONS

Social media platforms offer new possibilities to meet new people and develop different kinds of relationships, either romantic, sexual, or different degrees of friendship. Nevertheless, users may face a number of issues when interacting with strangers met online, such as lack of authenticity, social stigma for engaging in this practice, or safety risks, which include online harassment, identity theft, burglary, or sexual assault. In particular, physical safety issues were a concern to some female participants, especially in the context of the hospitality exchange experience in relation to potential sexual advances by male couchsurfers, which led some of them to decide to exchange hospitality with other women only. This moral panic is related to the fact that they knew about some female couchsurfers who had bad experiences, but also to the patriarchal discourse that dictates that women have to prevent unknown men from attacking them. This "stranger danger" myth, Baym (2010) argues, is not correlated with statistics, which show that most sexual attacks happen within environments that are familiar to the victim. As a good security measure, most female participants pointed to common sense and the need to observe whether the potential host or guest had a number of good references.

The preceding discussion shows that patriarchal gender roles are perpetuated through social media. In the case of Badoo, men usually started the conversations and women selected among the users who contacted them first. In addition, female Badoo users who started the conversations were considered "desperate", and those who had erotic pictures were labelled "sluts". There was also a gender clash in the expectations to participate on Badoo; participants claimed that most women wanted to find a partner, while most men wanted casual sex. This traditional scenario where women are pictured as lacking sexual desire while men are sexually obsessed was also reported on Badoo interaction. Although I am not sure to what extent this double sexual standard corresponds to reality or if participants just tried to fit into conventional expectations of their gender roles, it is clear that patriarchal gender roles are reproduced and reinforced online. As Illouz (2013) observes, male sexual power resides in the ability to perpetuate courtship rules, which may explain why male users tried to justify traditional gender roles as "natural" by using the expression "we are the hunters".

In this study participants showed acceptance of ephemeral contemporary ways of association as meaningful experiences. Social media platforms appeared as valid tools, mediums, or places to find new relationships, although most of them end up being short term. In particular, CouchSurfing (2018) appeared as a more successful platform than Badoo for finding both long-lasting friendships and partners. The few "good friends" participants found through Badoo or CouchSurfing were valued as the best experiences of participating on the sites, over romantic relationships. This finding fits with the trend towards an increasing importance of friendship within intimate life (e.g., Bauman 2003; Chambers 2006), which in many instances substitutes family relationships.

References

Alexa. (2018). *Traffic of Badoo.com*. http://www.alexa.com/siteinfo/badoo.com. Date Accessed 3 June 2018.

Bauman, Z. (2003). *Liquid love: On the frailty of human bonds*. Cambridge: Polity Press.

Baym, N. K. (2010). *Personal connection in the digital age*. Cambridge: Polity Press.

boyd, d. (2008). Facebook's privacy trainwreck: Exposure, invasion, and social convergence. *Convergence, 14*(1), 13–20.

boyd, d. (2010a). Social network sites as networked publics: Affordances, dynamics, and implications. In Z. Papacharissi (Ed.), *A networked self: identity, community, and culture on social network sites* (pp. 39–58). London: Routledge.

boyd, d. (2010b). Friendship. In M. Ito et al. (Eds.), *Digital research confidential: The secrets of studying behavior online* (pp. 79–115). Cambridge, MA: MIT Press.

Badoo. (2018). *Safety and security tips.* https://badoo.com/safetytips.phtml. Date Accessed 17 June 2018.

Bialski, P. (2013). Not on my couch. The limitations of sharing in the age of collaborative travel and hospitality networks. In *RC21 conference, 29/31 August 2013, Berlin.* http://www.rc21.org/conferences/berlin2013/RC21-Berlin-Papers/non%20pdf/31-Bialski.doc. Date Accessed 22 Feb 2014.

Brake, D. R. (2014). *Sharing our lives online: Risks and exposure in social media.* London: Palgrave Macmillan.

Chambers, D. (2006). *New social ties: Contemporary connections in a fragmented society.* Basingstoke: Palgrave Macmillan.

Chambers, D. (2013). *Social media and personal relationships: Online intimacies and networked friendship.* Basingstoke: Palgrave Macmillan.

CouchSurfing. (2018). *Terms of use.* http://www.couchsurfing.com/about/terms-of-use/. Date Accessed 8 June 2018.

Degim, I. A., & Johnson, J. (2015). Introduction. In I. A. Degim, J. Johnson, & T. Fu (Eds.), *Online courtship: Interpersonal interactions across borders* (pp. 1–16). Amsterdam: Institute of Network Cultures.

Driscoll, C. (2008). This is not a blog: Gender, intimacy, and community. *Feminist Media Studies, 8*(2), 197–224.

Ellison, N., Heino, R., & Gibbs, J. (2006). Managing impressions online: Self-presentation processes in the online dating environment. *Journal of Computer-Mediated Communication, 11*(2), 415–441.

Enguix, B., & Ardèvol, E. (2011). Enacting bodies: Online dating and new media practices. In K. Ross (Ed.), *The handbook of gender, sex and media* (pp. 502–515). Oxford: Wiley-Blackwell.

Germann Molz, J. (2012). CouchSurfing and network hospitality: "It's not just about the furniture". *Hospitality & Society, 1*(3), 215–225.

Giddens, A. (1992). *The transformation of intimacy: Sexuality, love and eroticism in modern societies.* Cambridge: Polity Press.

Gibbs, J. L., Ellison, N. B., & Lai, C. H. (2011). First comes love, then comes Google: An investigation of uncertainty reduction strategies and self-disclosure in online dating. *Communication Research, 38*(1), 70–100.

Hall, J. A., Park, N., Song, H., & Cody, M. J. (2010). Strategic misrepresentation in online dating: The effects of gender, self-monitoring, and personality traits. *Journal of Social and Personal Relationships, 27*(1), 117–135.

Haferkamp, N., Eimler, S. C., Papadakis, A. M., & Kruck, J. V. (2012). Men are from Mars, women are from Venus? Examining gender differences in self-presentation on social networking sites. *Cyberpsychology, Behavior, and Social Networking, 15*(2), 91–98.

Haraway, D. (1997). *Modest_Witness@Second_Millennium.FemaleMan©Meets_ OncoMouse™: Feminism and technoscience.* New York: Routledge.

Hearn, A. (2008). "Meat, mask, burden": Probing the contours of the branded "self". *Journal of Consumer Culture, 8*(2), 197–217.

Heino, R. D., Ellison, N. B., & Gibbs, J. L. (2010). Relationshopping: Investigating the market metaphor in online dating. *Journal of Social and Personal Relationships, 27*(4), 427–447.

Illouz, E. (2013). *Why love hurts: A sociological explanation.* Cambridge: Polity Press.

Jacobs, K. (2009). Is there life on adult FriendFinder? Sex and logic with the happy dictator. In: *Digital arts and culture: "After media: Ebodiment and context", 12/16 December 2009, Irvine.* http://escholarship.org/uc/item/1t91z25z. Date Accessed 9 Feb 2015.

Jamieson, L. (2013). Personal relationships, intimacy and the self in a mediated and global digital age. In K. Orton-Johnson & N. Prior (Eds.), *Digital sociology* (pp. 13–33). New York: Palgrave Macmillan.

Jamieson, L., Morgan, D., Crow, G., & Allan, G. (2006). Friends, neighbours and distant partners: Extending or decentring family relationships? *Sociological Research Online, 11*(3). http://www.socresonline.org.uk/11/3/jamieson. html. Date Accessed 9 Feb 2013.

Lambert, A. (2013). *Intimacy and friendship on Facebook.* Basingstoke: Palgrave Macmillan.

Leurs, K., & Ponzanesi, S. (2012). The performance of gender by migrant girls in instant messaging spaces. In K. Ross (Ed.), *Handbook of gender, sex and the media* (pp. 436–454). Hoboken: Wiley-Blackwell.

Marar, Z. (2012). *Intimacy.* London: Routledge.

Marar, Z. (2014). *Intimacy.* London: Routledge.

Martínez-Lirola, M. (2012). Aproximación a la interacción virtual: El caso de la red social Badoo. *Palabra Clave/Keyword, 15*(1), 107–127.

Marwick, A. E. (2013). *Status update: Celebrity, publicity, and branding in the social media age.* New Haven: Yale University Press.

Miguel, C. (2016). Visual intimacy on social media: From selfies to the co-construction of intimacies through shared pictures. *Social Media + Society, 2*(2), 1–10.

Miller, V. (2015). Resonance as a social phenomenon. *Sociological Research Online, 20*(2), 9. http://www.socresonline.org.uk/20/2/9.html. Date Accessed 19 Sept 2015.

Peter, J., & Valkenburg, P. M. (2007). Who looks for casual dates on the Internet? A test of the compensation and the recreation hypotheses. *New Media & Society, 9*(3), 455–474.

Plant, S. (1997). *Zeroes and ones: Digital women and the new technoculture.* London: Fourth Estate.

Rasmussen, L. (2014). Catfished: Exploring viewer perceptions of online relationships. In A. F. Slade, A. J. Narro, & B. P. Buchanan (Eds.), *Reality television: Oddities of culture* (pp. 237–248). Plymouth: Lexington Books.

Rosen, D., Roy Lafontaine, P., & Hendrickson, B. (2011). CouchSurfing: Belonging and trust in a globally cooperative online social network. *New Media & Society, 13*(6), 981–998.

Smith, A., & Anderson, M. (2016). 5 facts about online dating. *Pew Internet & American Life Project.* http://www.pewresearch.org/fact-tank/2016/02/29/5-facts-about-online-dating/#. Date Accessed 13 June 2018.

Tanenbaum, L. (2015). *I am not a slut: Slut-shaming in the age of the Internet.* New York: Harper Collins.

Thelwall, M. (2011). Privacy and gender in the social web. In S. Trepte & L. Reinecke (Eds.), *Privacy online: Perspectives on privacy and self-disclosure in the social web* (pp. 251–265). Heidelberg: Springer.

Tsatsou, P. (2012). The role of social culture in Internet adoption in Greece: Unpacking "I don't want to use the Internet" and frequency of use. *The Information Society, 28*(3), 174–188.

Van Doorn, N., & Van Zoonen, L. (2008). Theorizing gender and the Internet: Past, present, and future. In A. Chadwick & P. N. Howard (Eds.), *The Routledge handbook of Internet politics* (pp. 261–274). London: Routledge.

Wajcman, J. (2010). Feminist theories of technology. *Cambridge Journal of Economics, 34*(1), 143–152.

Whitty, M. T., & Buchanan, T. (2012). The online romance scam: A serious cyber-crime. *Cyberpsychology, Behavior, and Social Networking, 15*(3), 181–183.

Zelizer, V. A. (2009). *The purchase of intimacy.* Princeton: Princeton University Press.

CHAPTER 7

Conclusions: Networked Intimacy

Abstract This chapter presents the main conclusions of the research project about intimacy practices in the age of social media and elaborates the concept of networked intimacy. The study focused on (mediated) intimacy practices among adults (25–49 years old) through three different platforms (Badoo, CouchSurfing, and Facebook) to analyse how users create and maintain intimate relationships through social media. The project combined a critical analysis of the politics of platforms with users' perspectives of their intimacy practices through social media. The chapter synthesizes the empirical findings and locates the study in current academic debates.

Keywords Networked intimacy • Personal relationships • Privacy • Sex • Social media • Strangers

In recent years, there has been a growing debate about how the domestication of social media technologies plays an important role in the way people negotiate intimacy in their everyday life. Therefore, a main question arises: to what extent does the intimacy that exists on social media differ from that offline? In order to shed light upon this enquiry, there are three concepts that can be drawn together: boyd's (2010, p. 39) concept of *networked publics*, Papacharissi's (2010) notion of the *networked self* (2010, p. 307), and Rainie and Wellman's (2012) concept of *networked*

© The Author(s) 2018   125
C. Miguel, *Personal Relationships and Intimacy in the Age of Social
Media*, https://doi.org/10.1007/978-3-030-02062-0_7

individualism (2012, p. 3). I then use the term "networked intimacy" in order to conceptualize intimacy in the context of social media. First, boyd's (2010, p. 39) concept of *networked publics* helps to conceptualize networked intimacy because it recognizes that social media interactions are partly framed by platforms and their affordances. boyd (2010) argues that three dynamics render social media interaction complex: blurring of public and private, invisible audiences, and social convergence. Thus, social media reframe notions of public and private, boundaries which are considered central to intimacy. Building on this concept, Hinton and Hjorth (2013, p. 44) use the term "intimate publics" in order to suggest that affection acts as a sort of glue of users' engagement on *and* with the platform. Their term extends boyd's (2010) argument, highlighting the important role intimacy plays in the configuration of these digital publics. Together, these concepts prove useful to me in conceptualizing networked intimacy as a primary driver and result of social media interaction, operating within a digital environment that is dominated by specific affordances allowing for different kinds of publicity. Second, Papacharissi's (2010, p. 307) concept of the *networked self*, which relates to how the public display of social interactions helps co-construct one's identity online. Such co-construction adds another layer, which asks us to consider not only the content of the interaction, but also the subjective experiences that accompany this content, similarly shaping the concept of networked intimacy. In addition, Papacharissi (2010) highlights the flexibility offered by social media platforms in interpersonal interactions with diverse kinds of people, who might be geographically dispersed, belong to one or more different networks, and exert variable levels of intimacy. Likewise, Rainie and Wellman (2012) emphasize the flexibility and freedom that social media offer to decide where and with whom to interact. Such flexibility and freedom place agency with the user. Indeed, Rainie and Wellman (2012, p. 3) use the term *networked individualism* in order to describe the new type of social operating system that emerges from fragmented networks (as opposed to the traditional communities, e.g., the family, the neighbourhood), which were formed prior to the Internet, but have been exponentially enhanced given the advent of social media. Rainie and Wellman suggest that the social itself is reconfigured within the digital age. In this sense, Chambers (2013) highlights the ways in which social media affordances allowing choice and flexibility to connect with different kinds of people correspond to late-modern ideas of transformation and democratization of the concept of intimacy.

Taken together, these authors nuance the notion of networked intimacy so as to include the digital context, content, subjective experiences, power relations, and interaction. Moreover, they remind us that intimacy is both reconceptualized in a digital age *and* long-standing, embedded within existing practices and social norms. Indeed, this is not a radical transformation of the notion of intimacy, but an adaptation of intimate interaction to social media environments, which possess particular affordances. As Byam (2010, p. 59) acknowledged, "[P]eople appropriate media characteristics as resources to pursue social and relational goals." For me, the extent to which the intimacy that exists upon social media is different from that occurring offline touches the heart of these debates, not least because it directly addresses the presumptions surrounding intimacy as a concept, as well as the digital environment in which that concept is currently contested.

This book has addressed how people use social media to create and manage personal relationships, by discussing different topics such as issues of authenticity, social stigma, sexual double standards, security concerns, the quality of the mediated interactions and relationships initiated online, or the disclosure of intimate information on social media in front of networked publics. This study has been especially focused on the workings of mediated interaction and on the creation of new relationships, by using Badoo, CouchSurfing, and Facebook as case studies. In addition, because participants also used other social media services, I referred to other social media platforms on occasion. I argue that people who are open to creating new relationships through social media use different social media platforms, for example, CouchSurfing, MeetUp, and a range of dating/hook-up sites, such as Badoo or Tinder. In this book I have approached the study of intimacy practices through social media from a twofold perspective: I have looked at social media platforms as intimacy mediators (including the study of their design and business models), and I have also analysed users' intimacy practices and users' perceptions of intimate interaction through social media. In contrast to some critical studies about social media, which do not take into consideration users' agency, I incorporated users' perspectives in order to comprehend how users negotiate platforms' politics in the context of their intimacy practices, and how they understand the concepts of intimacy and privacy when interacting through social media.

One of the first issues I identified in the study of "networked intimacy" was a clash between the concepts of privacy and intimacy, since some authors used both terms interchangeably. Therefore, what would be the current difference between privacy and intimacy when interacting through social media? Although participants often clashed both terms as well, drawing on participants' perspectives, privacy can be defined as the state of control over personal information (confidentiality) or physical access to the person. Privacy also refers to the space where people can develop personal relationships apart from others, related to restricted access and trust towards the people allowed into that private sphere. Privacy was often defined as the opposite of publicity. With the extensive use of the Internet, privacy is becoming an increasingly socio-technical matter where personal information is persistent, replicable, and networked and can reach a large audience, which complicates the management and control of published information. On the other hand, intimacy refers to a sense of closeness within personal relationships, achieved by sharing inner thoughts and feelings. An intimate relationship is a kind of personal relationship that is subjectively experienced and can also be socially recognized as "close". The "closeness" indicated by intimacy is, to a certain extent, reciprocal and can have several dimensions: emotional, informational, and physical, although they can be interconnected and complement each other. In reference to the use of the word "intimacy" as a euphemism for sex, which especially male participants referred to, we should clarify that people can be intimate without having sex, and that sexual contact can occur without intimacy, as Jamieson (2012) observed. In addition, some participants related to intimacy as exclusive and dependent on trust. As we can see, the exclusivity and dependence on trust were common to privacy and intimacy definitions.

Intimacy has traditionally been shared and experienced in the private sphere. However, intimacy can be experienced in private or in public, although the commonly accepted rules of sociability seek to preserve intimacy in the private realm. In contemporary society, intimate lives can be represented and articulated in public areas (e.g., reality shows, the *camgirl* phenomenon, social media presence updated with intimate information). The public nature and extent of these practices of intimacy in the context of the media seem to contradict the secrecy and exclusivity that traditionally have defined intimacy. Social media companies have consciously participated in the transformation of social norms to encourage users to reveal more personal information under the imperative of "sharing" in order to monetize it for advertising purposes. In fact, in this study, most participants used the word "sharing" in order to specify self-disclosure through social media. Although intimacy in public gets high visibility for its disruptive nature, in this study, it was not a widespread practice among participants, in line with the research conducted by some scholars (e.g., Hogan 2010; Gürses and Díaz 2013; Young and Quan-Haase 2013), which showed that users tend to disclose only superficial information on their social media profiles to keep their social privacy. Most participants considered these expressions of intimacy in public to be inappropriate.

Defining what is considered intimate is a subjective matter, and it is further complicated when the interaction is through social media. There are certain types of personal information that people often expect to keep private. Sexual orientation and relationship status were the topics participants identified more often as intimate when interacting through social media. Other topics that participants considered intimate in the context of social media interaction included: sexual content, alcohol intake, political and religious beliefs, and emotions. The expectations of which information should remain private also varied from one platform to another; therefore, the decision to publish intimate information was contextual. These findings resonate with the concept of *contextual integrity* discussed by Nissenbaum (2009). Thus, participants who considered their sexual orientation to be intimate disclosed this information on Badoo but not on Facebook or CouchSurfing, the reason being that on these platforms, they did not consider it relevant, while on Badoo it was necessary to achieve the goal of meeting a potential (sexual) partner. LGTB participants were especially concerned about the revelation of their sexual orientation on Facebook because of the possibility to reach unintended audiences.

Trust was identified as a prerequisite for revealing personal information, and hence, to build intimacy through social media. In the context of online interaction between strangers, the lack of co-presence complicates the development of trust, as some scholars have argued (e.g., Vincent and Fortunati 2009; Wessels 2012). Participants mainly used Badoo and CouchSurfing to create new friendships and to find (sexual) partners. In order to foster a safe environment social media platforms where the interaction is among strangers have increasingly incorporated reputation and verification systems, or implement "real name policies" to try to certificate users' identity in order to provide a trustworthy and safe environment for the creation of new relationships.

Although the use of social media for meeting new people is increasingly becoming a common practice, as Hine (2015) observes, creating intimate relationships online is still stigmatized. There is a certain stigma attached to the use of dating sites, since users are often perceived as lacking social skills to meet people offline, to be only interested in sex, or to be desperate (e.g., Anderson 2005; Madden and Duggan 2013). In this study, social stigma for using social media to meet strangers online was identified as an issue (especially among male users), but it seemed to not affect most participants. Nevertheless, there were a range of authenticity and safety issues that participants reported to have experienced themselves or which they were concerned about, such as deceptive self-presentation, online harassment, sexual advances, robbery, and identity theft. In the case of Badoo some female participants reported that they had received unpleasant messages through the chat feature, some of these being sexist comments. Badoo took into account this issue, and permits blocking other users in order to avoid receiving unwanted messages. Also, when the interaction moves offline, users may face sexual harassment or robbery. There were mainly female participants who had experienced these kinds of problems as a result of interacting with people they had met through Badoo. These issues and bad experiences contributed to the lack of trust in other users, and led to some participants being very careful in the selection of the people they wanted to interact with. For this reason, I argue that social media platforms where people interact with strangers should implement better safety measures and policies to punish bad practices (e.g. misrepresentation) and harassers. For safety reasons, Badoo (2015) encourages users to conceal their full names and information that could identify them to protect themselves and interact with verified users. Nevertheless, more efforts can be done to improve the verification systems, like having to scan one's ID or passport in order to verify one's identity, like Airbnb (2018) does, especially in the case of CouchSurfing, since most concerns were formulated by female participants in relation to sexual harassment in the hospitality exchange experience.

When discussing social media data mining, most participants accepted the trade-off of data mining for free access to the service. Despite claims made by scholars about the exploitative nature of social media platforms and the lack of transparency about data mining (e.g., Van Dijck 2013; Fuchs 2014), most participants expressed their knowledge about customized advertising and the fairness of exchanging their navigation data for connectivity. Thus, as Jenkins et al. (2013) point out, the problem is not the presence of business models in social media environments, but the bad practices within them. In addition, most participants did not find problematic the intervention of money in the creation of new relationships, as they consider it a good investment in case of a positive outcome. In the case of Badoo, some of participants even recognized that they had interiorized the logics of the market and engaged in self-marketing strategies, since they were aware that the selection of the best pictures and smart descriptions would attract potential (sexual) partners.

In recent years the practice of courtship and flirting has increasingly moved online. The convergence of the ubiquitous presence of smartphones with mobile applications for dating, such as Tinder, Badoo, Grindr, Meetic, or PlentyOfFish, that allow users to geo-localize people nearby, is boosting this phenomenon. The immediacy and growing visuality are key to enabling the success of these applications. Dating/hook-up platforms are beneficial as long as they help in combating loneliness and finding a (sexual) partner. Nevertheless, most participants who used dating/hook-up platforms did not seem very pleased with the results. Many complained of the lack of response from women, the "poor quality" of the people who create a profile on these sites, and about the presence of fake profiles. Almost all participants generally agreed that female users seek a lasting relationship, while men seek sex, and these different expectations produce mutual dissatisfaction. I believe that some women also want sex, but they think they cannot express it openly for fear of being stigmatized. Findings seem to suggest that the patriarchal gender roles have not changed but are simply reproduced online because participants take their social/cultural assumptions online with them. Patriarchal double standards were observed on social media interaction, particularly in the context of courtship and flirting through Badoo. Most participants claimed that men usually started the conversations and women just chose among the men who had contacted them. The persistence of sexist double standards is the real problem in the whole dating scenario, both online and offline. As Giddens (1992) points out, the myth "Men want sex, women want love" has to be reconfigured in contemporary society (1992, p. 66). Badoo itself is not misogynist; society is. There are clearly sexual double standards operating in society, which are accentuated in these dating/hook-up sites, such as Badoo. Many men do not want to engage in serious romantic relationships with women they consider libertine, so they only seek short relationships or sex in these platforms.

Social media platforms offer new ways to meet people, which may often result in just acquaintances but, at the same time, can facilitate the creation of intimate relationships, for example, friends, partners, or hook-ups. The process of moving the interaction offline is much more difficult in the case of Badoo than on CouchSurfing. Although a few participants decided to stop using Badoo after bad experiences using the platform, many participants kept trying to meet interesting people. The hope for finding intimacy in the net, a "special" friend or partner, remains in participants' imaginaries, otherwise they would stop using these kinds of social media platforms. This does not imply that participants do not try to find meaningful relationships through other channels. Platforms such as Badoo and CouchSurfing, which are designed to connect with strangers, do not represent a massive change or a deep transformation in traditional intimacy practices, since it is clear that patriarchal gender roles are reproduced online, but they are just other tools that people use in their search for intimacy. It seems that friendship is increasingly valued within intimate relationships, which in many instances substitutes family relationships. As most participants were single and did not have children, they may use social media to find other kinds of meaningful associations, either long-lasting or transient. Ephemeral associations, such as hospitality exchange experiences or short-term friendships when travelling, were equally valued as positive and meaningful experiences in their lives. These shared "here and now" experiences, although fleeting and transient, still involve forms of intimacy.

REFERENCES

Airbnb. (2018). *What is verified ID?* https://www.airbnb.co.uk/help/article/450/what-is-verified-id. Date Accessed 9 June 2018.

Anderson, T. L. (2005). Relationships among Internet attitudes, Internet use, romantic beliefs, and perceptions of online romantic relationships. *CyberPsychology & Behavior, 8*(6), 521–531.

Badoo. (2015). *Safety and security tips.* [Online]. Available from: https://badoo.com/safetytips.phtml. Accessed 28 Dec 2015.

Baym, N. K. (2010). *Personal connection in the digital age.* Cambridge: Polity Press.

boyd, d. (2010). Social network sites as networked publics: Affordances, dynamics, and implications. In Z. Papacharissi (Ed.), *A networked self: identity, community, and culture on social network sites* (pp. 39–58). London: Routledge.

Chambers, D. (2013). *Social media and personal relationships: Online intimacies and networked friendship.* Basingstoke: Palgrave Macmillan.

Fuchs, C. (2014). *Social media: A critical introduction.* London: Sage Publications.

Giddens, A. (1992). *The transformation of intimacy: Sexuality, love and eroticism in modern societies.* Cambridge: Polity Press.

Gürses, S., & Díaz, C. (2013). Two tales of privacy in online social networks. *Security & Privacy, 11*(3), 29–37.

Hine, C. (2015). *Ethnography for the Internet: Embedded, embodied and everyday.* London: Bloomsbury Publishing.

Hinton, S., & Hjorth, L. (2013). *Understanding social media.* London: Sage Publications.

Hogan, B. (2010). The presentation of self in the age of social media: Distinguishing performances and exhibitions online. *Bulletin of Science, Technology & Society, 30*(6), 377–386.

Jamieson, L. (2012). Intimacy as a concept: Explaining social change in the context of globalisation or another form of ethnocentricism? *Sociological Research Online.* [Online], *1*(1). Available from: http://clarion.ind.in/index.php/clarion/article/view/11. Accessed 9 Feb 2013.

Jenkins, H., Ford, S., & Green, J. (2013). *Spreadable media: Creating value and meaning in a networked culture.* New York: New York University Press.

Madden, M., & Duggan, M. (2013). Online dating & relationships. *Pew Internet & American Life Project.* http://www.pewinternet.org/2013/10/21/online-dating-relationships/. Date Accessed 13 June 2018.

Nissenbaum, H. (2009). *Privacy in context: Technology, policy, and the integrity of social life.* Stanford: University Press.

Papacharissi, Z. (2010). *A Private sphere: Democracy in a digital age.* Cambridge, MA: Polity Press.

Rainie, H., & Wellman, B. (2012). *Networked: The new social operating system.* Cambridge, MA: MIT Press.

Van Dijck, J. (2013). *The culture of connectivity: A critical history of social media.* Oxford: Oxford University Press.

Vincent, J., & Fortunati, L. (2009). *Electronic emotion: The mediation of emotion via information and communication technologies.* Bern: Peter Lang.

Wessels, B. (2012). Identification and the practices of identity and privacy in everyday digital communication. *New Media & Society, 14*(8), 1–18.

Young, A. L., & Quan-Haase, A. (2013). Privacy protection strategies on Facebook: The Internet privacy paradox revisited. *Information, Communication & Society, 16*(4), 479–500.